The kingdom of God is not food and drink
but righteousness and peace and joy in the Holy Spirit.
(Romans 14:17)

KINGDOM MANIFESTO

A CALL TO JOYFUL ACTIVISM

RICK HOWE

BOOKS BY RICK HOWE

Path of Life: Finding the Joy You've Always Longed For, 2012, University Ministries Press Revised Edition, 2017. 279 pages.

River of Delights: Quenching Your Thirst For Joy, Volume 1, 2015, University Ministries Press Revised Edition, 2017. 230 pages.

River of Delights: Quenching Your Thirst For Joy, Volume 2, 2015, University Ministries Press Revised Edition, 2017. 250 pages.

Living Waters: Daily Refreshment for Joyful Living, 2017, University Ministries Press. 393 pages.

Reasons of the Heart: Joy and the Rationality of Faith, 2017, University Ministries Press. 250 pages.

FOR SMALL GROUP STUDIES

Enjoying God: Discovering the Greatest of All Pleasures, University Ministries Press, 2017. 122 pages.

Love's Delights: The Joys of Marriage and Family, University Ministries Press, 2017. 104 pages.

Sacred Patterns: Work, Rest, and Play in a Joyful Vision of Life, University Ministries Press, 2017. 122 pages.

Kingdom Manifesto: A Call to Joyful Activism, University Ministries Press, 2017. 104 pages.

Joy and the Problem of Evil, University Ministries Press, Boulder, 2017. 122 pages.

For more information, visit www.rickhowe.org.

UNIVERSITY MINISTRIES PRESS
BOULDER, COLORADO
Copyright © 2015.
University Ministries Press Edition, 2017.

This book represents materials from Rick Howe, *Rivers of Delight: Quenching Your Thirst For Joy, Volume 2* and *Path of Life: Finding the Joy You've Always Longed For* (Boulder, CO: University Ministries Press, Revised Editions, 2017) Used by Permission.

Scripture quotations are from The Holy Bible, English Standard Version® (ESV®), copyright © 2001 by Crossway, a publishing ministry of Good News Publishers. Used by permission. All rights reserved.

Scripture taken from the Holy Bible, NEW INTERNATIONAL VERSION®. Copyright © 1973, 1978, 1984 by Biblica, Inc. All rights reserved worldwide. Used by permission. NEW INTERNATIONAL VERSION® and NIV® are registered trademarks of Biblica, Inc. Use of either trademark for the offering of goods or services requires the prior written consent of Biblica US, Inc.

Revised Standard Version of the Bible, copyright ©1952 [2nd edition, 1971] by the Division of Christian Education of the National Council of the Churches of Christ in the United States of America. Used by permission. All rights reserved.

Any people depicted in stock imagery provided by iStockPhoto are models, and such images are being used for illustrative purposes only. Certain stock imagery © iStockPhoto.

ISBN: 978-0-9962696-4-3

ABBREVIATIONS

KJV   King James Version
NKJV   New King James Version
NIV   New International Version
NRSV   New Revised Standard Version

CONTENTS

AUTHOR'S NOTE

The material in *Kingdom Manifesto* is taken from my works, *Path of Life: Finding the Joy You've Always Longed For* and *River of Delights: Quenching Your Thirst For Joy, Volume 2.* I thought it would be worthwhile to put everything I've written about the Kingdom of God in one place for readers who wish to explore this very important topic on its own.

As you will see, there are many endnotes. If texts of Scripture are not given in full in the main body of a chapter, they have been included in the endnotes to make it possible for you to read the book without the extra chore of looking them up yourself. There are also many references to other works, as well as my own comments. My suggestion is that you read this work first without interacting with the endnotes to trace the flow of thought without interruption, and then read it again with those references.

The "Questions for Thought and Discussion" for each chapter reflect my hope that you will study this book with others, my belief that learning in community is the best way to learn, and my prayer that God will use this book to create communities of joy for the advancement of his Kingdom.

INTRODUCTION

Is it morally responsible for us to pursue joy in a world in which there is so much suffering? How can we seek joy when others live in poverty, are victims of violence and oppression, are ravaged by disease, or have been crushed beneath the weight of life? If a quest for joy meant flight from the world, I can't see how it would be permissible for us, and even less how it could be praiseworthy.

Whether it is entirely true or not, a common complaint against Christians is that we are so heavenly minded that we are of no earthly good. (In our day it would be truer to say that we are so earthly minded that we are of no earthly or heavenly good.[1]) Because some who profess Christian faith show little interest in making the world a better place, it is at least tempting to see a pursuit of joy as an explanation for their apathy toward the world in its distress.[2]

Those who flee the world and its problems to gain joy are not pursuing joy, but a counterfeit. Retreating from the world and its sorrow will not help them find the joy they are looking for. They won't find it because it can't be found that way. Joy is not a grail whose quest takes us away from others in their need; it is more like a magnetic force that draws us into their plight.

If we are to understand how joy relates to our troubled world, we must begin here: God has not instructed us how to live in the world from a position of ignorance about the world, disinterest in the world, or detachment from it. The world does not exist, nor does history move an inch in any direction, apart from his all-inclusive knowledge and sovereign purposes.[3] This includes the rise and demise of nations[4] as well as the sparrow that falls lifelessly to the ground.[5] The right place to begin is the observation that the God who commands us to live joyfully in the world is the same God who is sovereign over the world and its travail. Our pursuit of joy and our involvement in a suffering world are united under God.[6]

If we seek joy by ignoring or refusing to come to grips with suffering, whether it is our own or the pain of others, we will never find what we are looking for. Joy does not sacrifice realism for personal peace or pleasure. In the words of Archbishop Temple, "Christian joy and hope do not arise from an ignoring of the evil in the world, but from facing it at its worst."[7] When we turn to the pages of the New Testament, we see Jesus teaching his disciples to face adversity squarely and with joy, "Blessed are you when men revile you and persecute you and utter all kinds of evil against you on my account. Rejoice and be glad."[8] When they faced the persecution that Jesus said would come, we find his followers rejoicing "that they were counted worthy to suffer dishonor" for the name of Christ.[9] We learn from Paul's experience, "I rejoice in my sufferings."[10] We read James' words, "Count it all joy, my brothers, when you meet trials of various kinds."[11] We see Peter approaching life the same way, "Rejoice in so far as you share Christ's sufferings."[12]

Joy does not look away from suffering. It faces it head-on, without flinching, and then looks through it. Suffering is not entirely opaque; it is partly transparent. There is much that we cannot see, but we can see enough for joy.[13] Joy looks through the lens of suffering to see what God is seeking to do, and exults in this:

> More than that, we rejoice in our sufferings, knowing that suffering produces character. (Romans 5:3, RSV)

> You joyfully accepted the plundering of your property, since you knew that you yourselves had a better possession and an abiding one. (Hebrews 10:34, RSV)

> Count it all joy, my brothers, when you meet trials of various kinds, for you know that the testing of your faith produces steadfastness. (James 1:2-3, RSV)

Joy is ruthlessly realistic about the world we live in, but refuses to reach the same conclusions drawn by pessimists and fatalists. Because joy is illumined by a Light they do not have, it envisions possibilities for the world that they do not see and cannot entertain.

CHAPTER 1

INTRODUCTION TO THE KINGDOM

THE NEED FOR THE KINGDOM

*T*he *Fellowship of the Ring*, by J.R.R. Tolkien, begins with dire news.[1] The evil power that had been vanquished in ancient times was resurgent, growing in strength, bent on conquest and a reign of terror. The Dark Tower had been rebuilt in Mordor. In the words of Tolkien:

> From there the power was spreading far and wide, and away far east and south there were wars and growing fear. Orcs were multiplying again in the mountains. Trolls were abroad, no longer dull-witted, but cunning and armed with dreadful weapons. And there were murmured hints of creatures more terrible than all these, but they had no name.[2]

In time, news of these troubling developments reached the Shire, the home of small, peace-loving people known as hobbits. The news was frightening. They were not adventurers. They were not warriors. They had none of the qualities that make one equal to the challenge of perilous times. Of all the inhabitants of Middle Earth, they were the least likely candidates for heroism.

One day Gandalf, wizard and guardian of Middle Earth, appeared in the Shire to enlist Frodo, the hobbit, in the great conflict to come. As they sat together in Bag End, Frodo's earthen home, Gandalf told the hobbit about the dark and sinister things happening in the world outside the Shire. The history of Middle Earth seemed to be coming to a cataclysmic end in a final clash between good and evil.

This exchange between Frodo and Gandalf is classic. Upon hearing this disturbing news, Frodo said, "I wish it need not have happened in my time." "So do I," said Gandalf, "and so do all who live to see such times. But that is not for them to decide. All we have to decide is what to do with the time that is given us."[3]

I'm with Frodo: I wish the evil unleashed in the world hadn't happened in our day. You have only to read a week's worth of news to know the desperate problems facing our generation: The drumbeats of war. The threat of nuclear annihilation. Collapsing economies. Masses protesting in streets. Terrorism. Violence. Greed. Corruption. Fraud. Plundering of the earth and careless use of its resources. Hunger. Poverty. Injustice. Tyranny. Oppression. Abortion. Infanticide. Human trafficking and slavery. I lack strength of heart to speak of it all.

Sometimes I wish I had been born in an earlier generation. But I believe that Gandalf speaks for Christ: That is not my decision or yours. It is God's. What is given to us is a choice. We must decide how we will live our lives in a day when the challenges are so great.

"May your Kingdom come; may your will be done on earth as it is in heaven."[4] Many people in many places in many centuries have voiced these words and expressed this longing in prayer. This will be the earnest plea of millions today. Unless the risen and exalted Christ returns to the earth, it will be their supplication tomorrow. What is true of God's will in heaven is not yet true of conditions on the earth. When the new heavens and earth becomes our unending environment, our petition will turn to praise, and we will revel in the fullness and wonders of God's reign. Until then our hearts cry out for the Kingdom, and the Kingdom lays claim to our hearts. How we respond is the most significant choice we will make for ourselves and for our world.

A CLASH OF KINGDOMS

If we could part the curtains that hide the unseen spiritual realm and see what is behind the woes of our world, we would see a rejection of God and his ways. And behind that we would see his ancient adversary blinding eyes, hardening hearts, and stirring a pot of malice that spills into our world. He is known by many names in the Scriptures: Lucifer, Satan, the devil, the evil one, the tempter, the accuser, the dragon, the father of lies, the god of this world.[5] With legions of angelic beings who followed him in a primordial rebellion against God, he is bent on deflecting worship from God, defying the will of God, and destroying God's world. His kingdom is dark; his reign, sinister. His power is great; his rage, greater. In a hymn for the ages, Luther wrote of him: "For still our ancient foe doth seek to work us woe; his craft and power are great, and armed with cruel hate, on earth is not his equal."[6]

There are two kingdoms in conflict: the kingdom of darkness, and the Kingdom of God. In the words of the apostle Paul, "He has delivered us from the domain of darkness and transferred us to the kingdom of his beloved Son, in whom we have redemption, the forgiveness of sins."[7] Whether we wish it or not, the clash between these two kingdoms is the backdrop of our lives in this world.

In any war there are battlefields, battlefronts, and strongholds. Battlefields are anywhere that fighting is taking place. The entire cosmos is a battlefield. There is no safe place. C.S. Lewis wrote: "There is no neutral ground in the universe. Every square inch, every split second is claimed by God, and counterclaimed by Satan."[8]

A battlefront is where fighting is intense, and the outcome is undecided but strategically important. Battlefronts in our own day include marriage and the family, the sanctity of life, and high places of power and authority. It is the spiritual strife behind nationalism, tribalism, and terrorism. It is the destructive power behind drug trafficking and human trafficking. You will find a battlefront wherever the designs of God for our world are under fierce attack.

A stronghold was once a battlefield, then a battlefront, and now is a place where the enemy has become entrenched, empowered, and emboldened to carry out his stratagems. Hitler's Germany, Stalin's Soviet Union, Amin's Uganda, or, more recently, Rwanda, Darfur, and Jihadism come quickly to mind. But violence is not the only sign of a satanic stronghold. There are strongholds in our own country and many other post-Christian nations. Paul wrote:

> For though we walk in the flesh, we are not waging war according to the flesh. For the weapons of our warfare are not of the flesh but have divine power to destroy strongholds. We destroy *arguments* and every lofty *opinion* raised against the *knowledge* of God, and take every *thought* captive to obey Christ. (2 Corinthians 10:3-6)

When you think of strongholds, think of false, destructive ideas, whether they are espoused openly, covertly, or wrapped in words that make them seem benign. Think of big ideas, influential ideas, that dishonor God, flout his will, and destroy his intentions for the world. Then think of who or what lies behind the lies. Who promotes them? Hollywood, Madison Avenue, much of the media, places of higher education, many places in government and the corporate world, pornographers, and the video game industry. Religious organizations can hide strongholds of the enemy.

In this spiritual war we are called to be a resistance movement. Freedom fighters. The land of the King has been invaded and occupied by an alien force. True subjects of the King, we are tasked with resisting the usurper until all that belongs to our King *by right* becomes his *in fact*. We are summoned to venture onto battlefields, to engage the spiritual enemy on battlefronts, and to recapture strongholds held by our foe.

THE FUTURE AND PRESENT KINGDOM

Jesus said that one day our sorrow will turn to joy.[9] One day, joy will emerge from the chrysalis of the world's travail and fly on sun-gilded wings in the new heavens and the new earth. In that place there will be no sadness.[10] There will be no reason for sorrow. There will be no time or occasion for it. Joy will occupy every waking moment in a land where there is no sleep![11] It will be all joy and joy more glorious than our feeble minds can fathom and our stunted imaginations can entertain. With so much to break our hearts in this world, how do we keep from losing heart? Part of the answer is nurturing hope in what God will bring about at the end of days. The glory and joy God has promised us far outweighs the struggle and suffering we may now endure:

> So we do not lose heart. . . . For this slight momentary affliction is preparing for us an eternal weight of glory beyond all comparison. (2 Corinthians 4:16-17)

> I consider that the sufferings of this present time are not worth comparing with the glory that is to be revealed to us. (Romans 8:18)

Joy looks through our present suffering and anticipates this future glory.

If this is all there is, however, it is hard to see how it can do much more than give us strength to endure the harsh realities of our world. Should we just twiddle our thumbs and wait for God's Kingdom to come? No – and here is the other part of the answer – because the Kingdom of God is not merely future. In its fullness it is yet to come; however, Jesus came to inaugurate the Kingdom, to bring its blessings into our present experience in advance and anticipation of its consummation when he returns. [12] The Kingdom of God does not force us to choose between heaven and earth. We must choose both if we pray as Jesus taught us, "Your kingdom come, your will be done, on earth as it is in heaven."[13] There is not one Kingdom, which is future; nor are there two Kingdoms, one present and another future. There is one Kingdom, which is present (in inauguration) and future (in consummation), and which reflects God's will for the world.

THE GOSPEL OF THE KINGDOM

When Jesus began his public ministry, he stirred the air with the dramatic announcement: "The time has come; the kingdom of God is upon you; repent and believe in the gospel."[14] A new era dawned with the coming of the Christ. A new epoch began. History skidded around this turning point and moved in a new direction.

Ancient prophecies sprang to life in the words and deeds of Jesus:

> The Spirit of the Lord is upon me,
>   because he has anointed me
>   to preach good news to the poor.
> He has sent me to proclaim release to the captives
>   and recovering of sight to the blind,
>   to set at liberty those who are oppressed,
> to proclaim the acceptable year of the Lord. (Luke 4:18-21)[15]

In the words and deeds of Jesus the Supernatural and natural realms met. In that meeting lives were transformed, wounded hearts were mended, and broken bodies were healed. It was an incursion of the Kingdom of God. Yet to be acknowledged, the rightful King was staking his claim.

Jesus taught his followers to make this Kingdom prayer centermost in the way they lived in the world:

> Our Father in heaven,
>   hallowed be your name.
> *Your kingdom come,*
>   *your will be done,*
>   *on earth as it is in heaven.*
> Give us this day our daily bread,
>   and forgive us our debts,
>   as we also have forgiven our debtors.
> And lead us not into temptation,
>   but deliver us from evil.
> *For yours is the Kingdom, the power and glory, forever. Amen.*
> (Matthew 6:9-13)[16]

When Jesus preached it was to proclaim the Kingdom.[17] When he taught it was to expound the Kingdom.[18] When he spoke in parables it was to illustrate the Kingdom.[19] When he cast out demons it was warfare for the Kingdom.[20] When he healed it was to display the power of the Kingdom.[21] When he dispatched his disciples throughout the land, it was as emissaries of the Kingdom.[22] When he commissioned them before his departure, it was to take the Gospel of the Kingdom to the ends of the earth.[23] When he promised to build the Church, he gave it the authority of the Kingdom.[24] In the forty days between his resurrection and his ascension he spoke with his disciples about the Kingdom of God.[25]

What is the Kingdom of God? It is the dynamic reign of God breaking into history, bringing righteousness, peace, and joy – the boon of his empire.[26] Its fullness lies in the future.[27] One day "every knee will bow, and every tongue will confess that Jesus Christ is Lord, to the glory of God the Father."[28] When that happens, we will no longer pray for the Kingdom to come, for it will surround us on every side and govern all of life.

The Gospel of the Kingdom announces that the Kingdom of God entered the world in the life, death, and resurrection of Jesus Christ.[29] It arrived in advance of its final realization, and now is conquering evil, bringing forgiveness of sin and reconciliation with God, restoring relationships, healing broken bodies and wounded hearts, and bestowing the blessings of God's reign.[30] This is the salvation we embrace. This is the Gospel we proclaim. It is a far greater power from a much higher authority than anything in this fallen world. It changes people who in turn change history. It is the only hope for our world.

QUESTIONS FOR THOUGHT AND DISCUSSION

1. With the progress and prosperity brought about by the Industrial Revolution, it was popular to say in the 18th and 19th centuries, "Every day in every way, the world is getting better." Would you say that today? Do you know of many who would?

2. Where do you see spiritual battlefields, battlefronts, and strongholds in the world today? Do you think many Christians are in touch with the "clash of kingdoms?"

3. If you haven't seen the theme of the Kingdom of God in the New Testament before, how does this chapter change your perspective on the Gospel?

4. How does the section on Jesus and the Kingdom influence your understanding of his ministry?

5. How does the section on Jesus and the Kingdom influence your understanding of his teaching?

CHAPTER 2

UNDERSTANDING THE KINGDOM

THE KINGDOM OF GOD
AND KINGDOMS OF THE WORLD

Jesus did not entrust the future of his redemptive work to human governments. He acknowledged their God-given but limited authority in human affairs.[1] Like the apostle Paul after him, he knew that government can be an instrument of God in this fallen world, protecting the innocent, punishing wrongdoers, and promoting good, even though it is always fallible and often fails.[2] But governments received no commission from him. While God can and does make providential use of them in service to his Kingdom,[3] Jesus' plans for redemptive change were not contingent upon earthly rulers and regimes.[4] Why? Because the Kingdom of God operates in radically different ways than governments do. Jesus put it this way:

> You know that those who are considered rulers of the Gentiles lord it over them, and their great ones exercise authority over them. But it shall not be so among you. But whoever would be great among you must be your servant, and whoever would be first among you must be

slave of all. For even the Son of Man came not to be served but to serve, and to give his life as a ransom for many. (Mark 10:42-45)

The Cross is the scepter of our King. It is the emblem of his Kingdom. It is no empty symbol. Our Lord was tortured to death on one at the hands of earthly rulers.[5] (Every human government in every time and place would have killed Jesus. He would have been perceived as a threat to all of them, including ours. If we think otherwise, we have false views of Jesus and false beliefs about our government.) The Cross brings atonement to us, but it is also an inspiration for us. It gives us a model for living in the world. Christ's Kingdom turns the world right side up by turning it upside down. We save our lives only by losing them.[6] The greatest are least, and the least are greatest.[7] The wisdom of the world is folly in his realm.[8] The weak in his Kingdom shame the strong in the world.[9] Where Christ reigns, greatness is measured not by power, but by humble service. Significance is measured not by palaces or oval offices, but by sacrificial engagement with a broken world.

One day the kingdoms of the world will "become the Kingdom of our Lord, and of his Christ, and he shall reign forever and ever!"[10] We should pray and act now in ways that are shaped by this future reality in our quest for the Kingdom.[11] We should not, however, because Jesus did not, make the work of his Kingdom dependent upon the kingdoms of this world. It is a great folly and woe to the Kingdom when we identify the Kingdom of God with any political party, politician, or political agenda! This does not diminish the importance of government or civic involvement; it magnifies the Kingdom of God and its transformative role in the world.

Richard John Neuhaus deserves to be quoted at length:

> Jesus Christ is Lord. That is the first and final assertion Christians make about all of reality, including politics. Believers now assert by faith what one day will be manifest to the sight of all: every earthly sovereignty is subordinate to the sovereignty of Jesus Christ.

The Church is the community of believers who bear witness to that claim. Because the Church is pledged to the Kingdom proclaimed by Jesus, it must maintain a critical distance from all the kingdoms of the world, whether actual or proposed. Christians betray their Lord if, in theory or practice, they equate the Kingdom of God with any political, social, or economic order of this passing time. At best, such orders permit the proclamation of the Gospel of the Kingdom and approximate, in small part, the freedom, peace and justice for which we hope. At worst, such orders attempt to suppress the good news of the Kingdom and oppress human beings who are the object of divine love and promise.[12]

THE LOCATION OF THE KINGDOM

Some people envision the world with a Creator who exists in a realm above and beyond the world, who brought the world into being, but does not act directly in it. This is the view of Deism, which was in vogue in the 17th and 18th centuries in Europe, and among some intellectuals in colonial America.[13] If not by the same name, this is the perspective of many today, especially among the growing number of people who claim no religious affiliation.[14] It is fashionable to believe in the existence of God, but not in the presence and activity of God in the world (unless it meets our needs, advances our interests, and does so on our own terms, which is utter folly).[15]

Another path moves in the same direction and often leads to the same destination. Many Bible-believing, church-going people take spatial language in the Scriptures literally, and so have a vision of life in which God, angelic beings, and those who enjoy his presence in an afterlife are distant and remote from us. Heaven is where they are, and heaven is somewhere else. Somewhere far, far away.[16] Because of the great expanse between us, we worship God, but we should not expect to find him actively involved in our world.

This is a mistaken way of seeing the world. The Nicene Creed begins with this affirmation: "We believe in one God, the Father Almighty, maker of heaven and earth, of all things seen and unseen."[17] Our world includes seen and unseen dimensions, both made by God, both arenas in which he acts. The unseen realm is supernatural, but not unnatural. It is as natural as anything we connect with through our senses. It is simply invisible. It is transparent to our eyes. We do not see it. We see through it.[18]

The seen and unseen dimensions of the world are interrelated. They overlap. They are interwoven. They flow into each other.[19] We should see the Kingdom of God against this backdrop. The Kingdom surrounds us but is invisible to us. It is an unseen supernatural realm, entirely subject to God's powerful reign, interfacing with the physical, tangible realm. Both are part of the world in which we live. In the words of Jesus, "The kingdom of God is at hand."[20] It is "near."[21] It is "in your midst."[22] It has "come upon you."[23] It is God's dynamic reign wherever it holds sway.[24]

The clash of kingdoms involves the world around us that is unseen to us. The "heavenly realms," or "heavenlies,"[25] are not somewhere else. They are here. The "principalities and powers" in these heavenly places are dangerous forces in our world, and all the more so because we cannot see them. The far more powerful reign of Christ is not exercised remotely. It is here – he is here – simply in a sphere that lies beyond our senses. We are surrounded by a "cloud of witnesses"[26] – the people of God who have gone before us. That gallery is here, simply in a dimension that is intangible to us.[27] (The faithful who have passed from the tangible world live in complete safety and joy not because they are far from this world, but because no evil may enter the unseen realm where the risen, reigning Christ is present to them at all times.)

This helps us understand why Jesus said, "Unless you are born of the Spirit, you cannot see the Kingdom of God."[28] It is not a physical seeing; it is a spiritual illumination. It is seeing with the "eyes of our hearts."[29] It is the discernment of spiritual realities in which we are enveloped.

Why is this important to Kingdom activists? Because imagining the Kingdom as far away, but requiring our action in the world on its behalf, is misguided. There is strength and courage in knowing that Kingdom realities are all around us, simply invisible to us. We connect with the supernatural just as surely as we do the natural.[30] We ourselves are part of both.[31] The world is enchanted with the supernatural, and we are part of the enchantment. Our prayers for the Kingdom don't have to reach to the heavens somewhere above us. God is near, and hears the quiet rustling of our hearts. Whispers are powerful in the Kingdom. Even sighs can be potent. We are not alone when we act for the Kingdom. Though unseen to us, the King is present with us, and he and his powerful emissaries are ready to engage in the battle for us.

ENTERING THE KINGDOM

The Kingdom of God is not a place, but we must still enter it.[32] Jesus said so, and he knows better than anyone. The gateway to the Kingdom is repentance and faith. Again, Jesus said so, and he should know: "Now after John was arrested, Jesus came into Galilee, proclaiming the gospel of God, and saying, 'The time is fulfilled, and the kingdom of God is at hand; repent and believe in the gospel.'"[33]

To enter the Kingdom we must cross a threshold. The first step is repentance: embracing radically new and different ways of thinking about God and ourselves.[34] We have falsely imagined God. We have believed that he is indifferent to our sin, and that he will indulge us in our sinfulness. In truth, he is altogether righteous and burns with a pure and wholesome hatred of all that is not. Because we have misunderstood God, we have also nurtured false views of ourselves. The ease with which we accommodate sin in our hearts leads us to believe that our condition is natural, normal, and acceptable. Not so! In the highest and purest sense of the word, God is holy, and, in the starkest contrast imaginable, we are not. We are crooked. Bent. Polluted. Stained. Guilty. Worthy of condemnation. Repentance lets the truth about God and ourselves pierce our hearts with sorrow – not feeling sorry for ourselves, but lamenting the sin that is a monumental affront to God.

Our false understanding of God not only underestimates his righteousness and its unrelenting demands, it understates his boundless love and desire to bless. In our distorted vision, we see him as grudging, stinting, loath to part with his hoard. Our false god is utterly unlike God as Jesus understood him. The true God is like the father whose prodigal son returns in repentance, who sees his son from a distance, is moved with compassion, runs to embrace and kiss his boy, and celebrates his return with music, dancing, and a great feast.[35]

In repentance we turn from sinful thoughts, affections, words, and deeds that alienate us from God and create a world filled with idols – false gods, every one. In faith, our second step into the Kingdom, we turn to the living and true God.[36] The bad news (for us) is that God is implacably hostile to all that is antithetical to his character and incompatible with his purposes. The good news (for us) is that his hostility is "not to the sinner but to the sin."[37] He loves sinners. He forgives repentant sinners. He welcomes them as friends. He invites them into a fellowship of love. He relates to them in grace and mercy, and gifts them with righteousness, peace, and unspeakable joy. This is the good news of the Kingdom. This is the favor of the King. Faith is the heart that is open and the hand that receives all that God is prepared to give.

Repentance and faith are our first steps into the Kingdom and then a way of living in the Kingdom.[38] They orient us to God and his concerns and desires for us. They are relational dispositions, tuning our hearts to God's. They are transformative practices, breaking the power of sin and creating an environment in our hearts in which the fruit of God's Spirit can grow.[39] And they are essential to our witness in the world, keeping us humble with the recognition of our own fallenness and need, grateful for the gracious riches of God's love in Christ, and joyful in the undeserved life we live under God's reign.

THE POWER OF THE KINGDOM

Talk is cheap. Anyone can speak words about the Kingdom. The Kingdom of God, however, is not about words, but life-transforming, world-changing vitality. The apostle Paul wrote: "The kingdom of God does not consist in talk but in power."[40]   The power of God's Kingdom breaks the status quo and brings new realities into being. It moves events in different directions, with different outcomes, than would have been the case if they were left to themselves.

No one has wielded this force like Jesus did: "God anointed Jesus of Nazareth with the Holy Spirit and with power. He went about doing good and healing all who were oppressed by the devil, for God was with him."[41] Now, we may believe this about Jesus, but the surprising claim of the New Testament is that this same power to do good, to bring healing and liberation to those who live under the sway of the evil one, can work in and through those who follow him:

> Behold, I am sending the promise of my Father upon you. But stay
> in the city until you are clothed with power from on high. (Luke
> 24:49)

Truly, truly, I say to you, whoever believes in me will also do the works that I do; and greater works than these will he do, because I am going to the Father. (John 14:12)

But you will receive power when the Holy Spirit has come upon you, and you will be my witnesses in Jerusalem and in all Judea and Samaria, and to the end of the earth. (Acts 1:8)

With great power the apostles were giving their testimony to the resurrection of the Lord Jesus, and great grace was upon them all. (Acts 4:33)

Stephen, full of grace and power, was doing great wonders and signs among the people. (Acts 6:8)

But we have this treasure in jars of clay, to show that the surpassing power belongs to God and not to us. (2 Corinthians 4:7)

Now to him who is able to do far more abundantly than all that we ask or think, according to the power at work within us, to him be glory in the church and in Christ Jesus throughout all generations, forever and ever. Amen. (Ephesians 3:20-21)[42]

The Kingdom of God surrounds us and is present in every moment. As we align our thoughts, affections, and decisions with God's rule, the Kingdom permeates us. As we become radically open to what God wants to do through us in the world, it empowers us. As we step out in our weakness, in obedient faith, it changes the world through us. Through us God's Kingdom comes and his will is done on the earth. Through us God breaks the status quo of human fallenness and brings new things into being. Through us healing, restoration, reconciliation, righteousness, peace, and joy come into the world.

The power of the Kingdom is not untethered energy swirling through the world, waiting for us to use. It is subject to God's rule and serves his purposes. Always. This might lead you to think that the power of the Kingdom has little to do with you, but that would be a false conclusion. It has everything to do with you and me, because God has chosen to exert his power in the world through our weakness when we respond to him in obedient faith. God intends this power to work through us as we are shaped by Christ and our lives are harnessed to the interests and concerns of the Kingdom. In fact, you can't be an agent of the Kingdom without enlisting for this possibility and looking for opportunities to be used by God in whatever ways he chooses for you.

THE WEAPONRY OF THE KINGDOM

How do we fight in the clash of kingdoms? Not with weapons the tangible world would recognize and fear. The apostle Paul described the armaments and accoutrements of spiritual warfare in his letter to the church in Ephesus:

> Finally, be strong in the Lord and in the strength of his might. Put on the whole armor of God, that you may be able to stand against the schemes of the devil. For we do not wrestle against flesh and blood, but against the rulers, against the authorities, against the cosmic powers over this present darkness, against the spiritual forces of evil in the heavenly places. Therefore take up the whole armor of God, that you may be able to withstand in the evil day, and having done all, to stand firm. Stand therefore, having fastened on the belt of truth, and having put on the breastplate of righteousness, and, as shoes for your feet, having put on the readiness given by the gospel of peace. In all circumstances take up the shield of faith, with which you can extinguish all the flaming darts of the evil one; and take the helmet of salvation, and the sword of the Spirit, which is the word of God, praying at all times in the Spirit, with all prayer and supplication. (Ephesians 6:10-16)

This battle must be fought beneath the banner of the Cross. We become dangerous for Christ and dangerous to his adversaries when we have so fully embraced his Cross-shaped love, when we hold it so tightly as the guiding truth and power of our lives, that all other things – including our own lives – seem as nothing compared to the greatness of his redeeming love:

> And I heard a loud voice in heaven, saying, "Now the salvation and the power and the kingdom of our God and the authority of his Christ have come, for the accuser of our brothers has been thrown down, who accuses them day and night before our God. And they have conquered him by the blood of the Lamb and by the word of their testimony, for they loved not their lives even unto death. (Revelation 12:10-11)

What does joy have to do with spiritual warfare? It is a powerful weapon. I wrote in *Path of Life*:

> Where God is, there is joy.

> If we knew the true nature and dimensions of joy, we would see that it is always, and never less than, our heart's encounter with the Joyful One.[43]

This is what makes joy so potent in the clash of kingdoms: The King himself is in it. Joy is one of the signs of God's Kingdom at work in the world.[44] His adversary knows this and so hates everything that has to do with joy. It is wretched to him. He hates the sounds of joy. He detests its music. He abhors its merriment. Luther said that the devil "cannot stand gaiety."[45] He can't abide it. He is undone by it. He must flee the field whenever true joy steps onto it. If this is so, then I say, "Let him feel the keen edge of our blades of joy![46] Let us march joyfully into the fray!"

QUESTIONS FOR THOUGHT AND DISCUSSION

1. How do you see the relationship between the Kingdom of God and human governments? What are the implications?

2. How does the section on "The Location of the Kingdom" challenge the way you have understood the world, and the relationship between the natural and supernatural realms?

3. How does this chapter challenge your understanding of repentance and faith and their role in the Christian life?

4. Talk about this quote in the context of your own life:

   > God intends this power to work through us as we are shaped by Christ and our lives are harnessed to the interests and concerns of the Kingdom. In fact, you can't be an agent of the Kingdom without enlisting for this possibility and looking for opportunities to be used by God in whatever ways he chooses for you.

5. The Church is too often known for its belligerence toward the world. How does this chapter's discussion of the weaponry of the Kingdom challenge this? How might it change this?

CHAPTER 3

THE KINGDOM AT WORK

PRAYING FOR THE KINGDOM

O ur first action for the Kingdom must be on bended knee. This must be first in our priorities and first in our deeds for the Kingdom, every day, throughout the day, in our hearts if not on our knees. Praying for the Kingdom reminds us that it is God's reign and not ours to which we have committed ourselves. He is our Sovereign, our Lord, our King. We are his servants, his subjects, his people. Our hands and feet serve his government, but his shoulders bear it.[1] His head wears its crown. All that we do for the Kingdom, we do at his bidding, for his greater glory in the world.

> Our Father in heaven,
> hallowed be your name.
> Your Kingdom come,
> your will be done,
>   on earth as it is in heaven.
> Give us this day our daily bread,
>   and forgive us our debts,
>   as we also have forgiven our debtors.
> And lead us not into temptation,

but deliver us from evil.
For yours is the Kingdom, the power and glory, forever. Amen.
(Matthew 6:9-13)[2]

Let this be your daily prayer. Pray it in full. Pray it in part. Let it be words on your tongue, thoughts in your mind, the silent focus of your heart. Let it be a whisper, a sigh, the direction of your desires – unspoken but fully disclosed to the One who knows all hearts and hears all prayer. Live here. Live this.

You can fill your life with well-intentioned deeds without this prayer, but it won't be agency for the Kingdom. It won't be fruitful for the Kingdom. It won't be the Kingdom of God working through you in the world.[3] You can busy yourself with well-intentioned activity, but you won't discern the will of God and participate in what he is doing. Pray, and you will.

KINGDOM RIGHTEOUSNESS, PEACE, AND JOY

If we answer the summons to be agents of the Kingdom, what is it that we are called to do? The apostle Paul gives us our clue: "The kingdom of God is not food and drink but righteousness and peace and joy in the Holy Spirit,"[4] We are called to pursue righteousness, peace, and joy in the Holy Spirit. It is not embracing an ideology, advancing the agenda of any political party, or protecting or expanding the interests of any tribe or nation. God is not a partisan.[5] His Kingdom rules over all. It is meant for all. Righteousness, peace, and joy in the Holy Spirit are supernatural forces that can work in and through us to transform the world and bring the will of God to the earth as it now is found in heaven.

What are these traits, and how are they related to the Kingdom? Some commentators see them as "the inward graces of the Spirit."[6] You can find that in other places in Paul's writing, but not here. Paul is addressing the way Christians live together in community, and the significance of the Kingdom of God for this. Righteousness, peace, and joy are what the Kingdom is about. They describe the culture of the Kingdom. They are the foreign and domestic policies of the Kingdom. They represent the Kingdom-in-action, empowered by God's Spirit. They are not what we hope to find when we look within; they are what we should expect to find when we see God's people living together – in the power of the Spirit – as representatives of God's Kingdom in the world. They are spheres of service, as Paul says next: "For the one who serves Christ in this is pleasing to God and approved by men."[7] As followers of Christ we are called to be agents of righteousness, ambassadors of peace, and heralds of joy. If we are fighting with each other over scruples, as they were in Rome, we cannot fulfill these Kingdom roles – which is exactly Paul's point.[8]

Kingdom righteousness in this context is not "the status of righteousness before God which is God's gift."[9] It is "righteous action"[10] or what biblical writers referred to as "doing righteousness."[11] It is action taken to promote and protect the well-being of others.[12] The righteousness of the Kingdom is what the Psalmist thought of when he said of God, "Righteousness and justice are the foundation of his throne."[13] God is committed to a world in which his creatures truly thrive. Ancient people of faith often praised God for his commitment to those who were least likely to flourish in a fallen, sinful world. We practice the righteousness of the Kingdom when our hearts align with God's, and we join him in seeking the good of others – especially those who need our help if they are to prosper in life:[14]

> He executes justice for the fatherless and the widow,
> and loves the sojourner, giving him food and clothing.
> (Deuteronomy 10:18)

> The LORD works vindication
>   and justice for all who are oppressed. (Psalm 103:6)

Happy is he whose help is the God of Jacob,
    whose hope is in the LORD his God,
    who made heaven and earth,
        the sea, and all that is in them;
    who keeps faith for ever;
        who executes justice for the oppressed;
    who gives food to the hungry.
The LORD sets the prisoners free;
    the LORD opens the eyes of the blind,
    the LORD lifts up those who are bowed down;
    the LORD loves the righteous.
The LORD watches over the sojourners,
    he upholds the widow and the fatherless;
    but the way of the wicked he brings to ruin.
The LORD will reign for ever,
    thy God, O Zion, to all generations.
Praise the LORD! (Psalm 146:5-10)

Righteous people are actively committed to the welfare of others:

I delivered the poor who cried,
    and the fatherless who had none to help him.
The blessing of him who was about to perish came upon me,
    and I caused the widow's heart to sing for joy.
I put on righteousness, and it clothed me;
    my justice was like a robe and a turban.
I was eyes to the blind,
    and feet to the lame.
I was a father to the poor,
    and I searched out the cause of him whom I did not know.
I broke the fangs of the unrighteous,
    and made him drop his prey from his teeth." (Job 29:12-17)

The righteous care about justice for the poor. (Proverbs 29:7, NIV)

Then the righteous will answer him, "Lord, when did we see you hungry and feed you, or thirsty and give you something to drink? When did we see you a stranger and invite you in, or needing clothes and clothe you? When did we see you sick or in prison and go to visit you?" The King will reply, "I tell you the truth, whatever you did for one of the least of these brothers of mine, you did for me." (Matthew 25:34-40)[15]

Then I heard what seemed to be the voice of a great multitude, like the roar of many waters and like the sound of mighty peals of thunder, crying out,

> "Hallelujah!
> For the Lord our God
>   the Almighty reigns.
> Let us rejoice and exult
>   and give him the glory,
> for the marriage of the Lamb has come,
>   and his Bride has made herself ready;
> it was granted her to clothe herself
>   with fine linen, bright and pure"—
> for the fine linen is the righteous deeds of the saints.
> (Revelation 19:6-8, ESV)

Those who have been brought into a right relationship with God long to see others join them. They yearn to see others flourish in God's will.[16] They eagerly share with all whose hearts are open, but seek the oppressed, the hungry, the poor, the fettered, the crippled, the deaf, and the blind, because they know that God is committed to them and their plight. They long to see them discover their help in the God of Jacob and their hope in the LORD their God. They take great pleasure in joining God in what he is doing, becoming the voice through which he speaks and the hands with which he touches people in need. This is the righteousness of the Kingdom. It must be important to followers of Jesus, because it was important to him.[17] He saw this as the heart of his mission, fulfilling the ancient prophecy:

> The Spirit of the Lord is upon me,
> because he has anointed me to preach good news to the poor.
> He has sent me to proclaim release to the captives
> and recovering of sight to the blind,
> to set at liberty those who are oppressed,
> to proclaim the acceptable year of the Lord. (Luke 4:18-19)

What about Kingdom peace? Again, it is tempting to see this as an experience of inner tranquility. But this moves us further from Paul's thought in this context. There are times when he is thinking about peace between people. Sometimes it is peace between fellow believers.[18] Sometimes it includes all who enter the circle of our lives: "If possible, so far as it depends on you, live peaceably with all."[19] When peace is put into the context of God's Kingdom, however, its boundaries are as broad as his reign. It is global in its design and intent. It is a harmony in the world that emerges from right relationships – with God, our neighbor, and the created order in which we have been placed. Because they have been introduced to this peace, people of the Kingdom are peacemakers. They seek to resolve conflict, to end strife, and to guide others into relational health. Before a world that is always watching, they model the possibilities of flourishing in life together.

Kingdom peace is the fulfillment of what the prophets called *shalom*: life at its best under God. Shalom describes health, well-being, fulfillment, harmony, and an environment of joy for all.[20] Cornelius Plantinga writes:

> The webbing together of God, humans, and all creation in justice,
> fulfillment, and delight is what the Hebrew prophets call *shalom*.
> We call it peace but it means far more than mere peace of mind or

a cease-fire between enemies. In the Bible, shalom means *universal flourishing, wholeness and delight* – a rich state of affairs in which natural needs are satisfied and natural gifts fruitfully employed, a state of affairs that inspires joyful wonder as its Creator and Savior opens doors and welcomes the creatures in whom he delights. Shalom, in other words, is the way things ought to be.[21]

There is a reason why joy follows righteousness and peace in this Kingdom triumvirate. How could we rejoice in a world without them? Such joy would be "insulted and undone."[22] If we are living in right relationships with God and with others, peace is the harmony that results,[23] and joy is our pleasure in that concord.

> Joy is what humans experience when the way the world is and the way the world ought to be converge. For Christians joy is love's delight in God and God's promised kingdom, when the way the world is and the way God wills the world converge.[24]

This is healthy joy. This is the joy God seeks for us.[25] One day it will fill the earth.

The righteousness, peace, and joy of the Kingdom are an indicative and an imperative for followers of Jesus.[26] To say that they are indicative of the Kingdom means that they are depictions of the life we enjoy under God's reign (in part now and fully in the future). To say that they are an imperative means that they are objectives which our King commands us to pursue as citizens of his Kingdom. Or we can put it this way: The righteousness, peace, and joy of God's Kingdom are a description and a demand. They are ways of describing the blessings of God's Kingdom we enjoy as its citizens, and at the same time they demand the investment of our lives as agents of the Kingdom in the world. They are both portrait and project. They portray Kingdom life, and are also the chief project, or enterprise, of the Kingdom. Righteousness, peace, and joy in the Holy Spirit will be perfectly realized in God's Kingdom in the age to come. Knowing that they will one day be our full possession, they become our goal in the present as we seek to live under God's sovereign and gracious reign.[27]

If we answer the call to be agents of God's Kingdom in the world, these are the objectives that will captivate our hearts and focus our energy. Whatever our strategies and tactics – which will be as many and varied as the situations in which we find ourselves – they will serve the greater goals of spreading righteousness, peace, and joy throughout the world.[28]

GOOD WORKS AND THE KINGDOM

In the first half of the last century there was a heated dispute in the United States between conservative and liberal Christians about how to understand the Gospel and its social implications. Liberals accused conservatives of privatizing the Gospel and making it socially irrelevant. Conservatives accused liberals of abandoning the Cross, pandering to modernity, and creating a new and different social Gospel in a vain attempt to bring the Kingdom of God through good works.[29]

The World War II generation (my parents) went to Christian colleges and seminaries that were embroiled in this controversy. Lines were drawn, words became weapons, and the world looked on in bemusement at the internecine battle. The next generation - my own – was raised believing that we had to choose sides in this clash. Our grandparents' and parents' fight had to become our own. Then the 1960s happened, and we questioned their conflicts and the values and beliefs that led to them.

In our adult years, many Christians in my generation have come to believe that both sides of this controversy were right in what they affirmed, and wrong in what they denied.[30]   Conservatives were right in affirming the centrality of the Cross in God's plan of redemption, and the necessity of a personal response of faith, but wrong in denying that this has social implications. [31] Liberals were right in seeing and insisting on those implications, but wrong in denying the importance of personal faith, and the role of the Cross in our salvation.

Followers of Jesus in the next generation (my children) don't understand why earlier generations of Christians fought about these things. They embrace the personal and social dimensions of the Gospel and can't fathom how this could be seen as a problem!

We are called to seek the Kingdom of God and to do good works.[32] They are united in God himself:

> *Your kingdom* is an everlasting kingdom,
>   and your dominion endures throughout all generations.
> The LORD is faithful in all his words
>   *and kind in all his works.*
> The LORD upholds all who are falling
>   and raises up all who are bowed down. (Psalm 145:13-14)

Good works don't bring the Kingdom. They don't build the Kingdom. They are a way of living in the Kingdom, for the Kingdom. They reflect the kindness of our King, and the congeniality of our hearts with his. When early followers of Jesus told his story to others, the Cross and good works were united in their tale:

> You know what has happened throughout the province of Judea, beginning in Galilee after the baptism that John preached — how God anointed Jesus of Nazareth with the Holy Spirit and power, and how *he went around doing good* and healing all who were under the power of the devil, because God was with him. We are witnesses of everything he did in the country of the Jews and in

Jerusalem. *They killed him by hanging him on a cross.* (Acts 10:37-39)

Jesus saw good works as a sign of the present Kingdom, and as evidence of citizenship in his eternal Kingdom:

> When the Son of Man comes in his glory, and all the angels with him, then he will sit on his glorious throne. Before him will be gathered all the nations, and he will separate people one from another as a shepherd separates the sheep from the goats. And he will place the sheep on his right, but the goats on the left. Then the King will say to those on his right, "Come, you who are blessed by my Father, inherit the kingdom prepared for you from the foundation of the world. For I was hungry and you gave me food, I was thirsty and you gave me drink, I was a stranger and you welcomed me, I was naked and you clothed me, I was sick and you visited me, I was in prison and you came to me." Then the righteous will answer him, saying, "Lord, when did we see you hungry and feed you, or thirsty and give you drink? And when did we see you a stranger and welcome you, or naked and clothe you? And when did we see you sick or in prison and visit you?" And the King will answer them, "Truly, I say to you, as you did it to one of the least of these my brothers, you did it to me." (Matthew 24: 31-40)

Good works have never saved anyone, but they are the point, purpose, and outward proof of our salvation. The apostle Paul put it this way:

> For by grace you have been saved through faith. And this is not your own doing; it is the gift of God, not a result of works, so that no one may boast. For we are his workmanship, created in Christ Jesus for good works, which God prepared beforehand, that we should walk in them. (Ephesians 2:8-10)

When good works are shaped by the Kingdom objectives of righteousness, peace, and joy in the Holy Spirit, and are done by people who model these traits in this power, the possibilities of transformed lives and a transformed world are greater than any of us can imagine.

NO FROWNING SAINTS!

If we are to be agents of joy in the world, this suggests something about us. The joy of others cannot be not isolated from our own. It is a shared joy.[33] We can only give what we have. As we give we receive. Not only is it unlikely that we will reach out to others in need if we are strangers to joy,[34] seeking the well-being of others grudgingly and reluctantly is a spiritual contradiction.[35] Paul saw this clearly:

> If you are helping others in distress, do it cheerfully. (Romans 12:8)[36]

> Each one must do as he has made up his mind, not reluctantly or under compulsion, for God loves a cheerful giver. (2 Corinthians 9:7)[37]

> Their abundance of joy and their extreme poverty have overflowed in a wealth of liberality on their part. (2 Corinthians 8:2)

Perhaps no one in recent memory has exemplified joyful compassion more than Mother Teresa. Malcolm Muggeridge described his experience with her:

> Accompanying Mother Teresa, as we did, to these different activities for the purpose of filming them – to the Home for the Dying, to the lepers and unwanted children, I found I went through three phases. The first was horror mixed with pity, the second compassion pure and simple, and the third, reaching far beyond compassion, something I had never experienced before – an

awareness that these dying and derelict men and women, these lepers with stumps instead of hands, these unwanted children, were not pitiable, repulsive or forlorn, but rather dear and delightful; as it might be, friends of long standing, brothers and sisters.[38]

He wrote of Mother Teresa and her co-workers:

Their life is tough and austere by worldly standards, certainly; yet I never met such delightful, happy women, or such an atmosphere of joy as they create. Mother Teresa, as she is fond of explaining, attaches the utmost importance to this joyousness. The poor, she says, deserve not just service and dedication, but also the joy that belongs to human love. This is what the Sisters give them abundantly.[39]

Imagine a world in which the Church across the globe is filled with joyful, compassionate people: men and women, girls and boys, whose loving action fills them with delight, whose joy overflows the cup of their own lives and spills onto needy people with a life-changing splash of grace. Imagine a world in which the Church in every country is empowered by the Holy Spirit and devoted to righteousness, peace, and joy. Imagine a world in which people from every nation, tribe, and tongue see our good works, done with joyful hearts, and glorify our Father in heaven. Jesus envisioned this for us.[40] How will you respond?

QUESTIONS FOR THOUGHT AND DISCUSSION

1. How does the Lord's Prayer factor into your daily life and the way you see and respond to events around you? How can you bring this prayer into your life in new ways?

2. Discuss this chapter's understanding of Kingdom righteousness, peace, and joy, and how this shapes your understanding of what God is seeking to do in the world.

3. What would it look like for you to pursue righteousness, peace, and joy? What would change for you?

4. How did you understand the role of good works in the Christian life before reading this chapter? Has anything changed after reading it? If so, what? What difference does it make?

5. How does joy lead to good works? How can good works be shaped by joy? How do you see this in Mother Theresa? How can you pursue this yourself, and encourage it in others?

CHAPTER 4

KINGDOM AGENTS

THE SUMMONING

If we have embraced Christ in faith, we are children of the King. Because of what Christ has done for us, we have been adopted into a royal family.[1] God is our Father; Christ, our brother.[2] We've been given a place of nobility – indeed, royalty – at the King's table. There is a regal inheritance in store for us beyond all that we can imagine.[3] With each new day we should celebrate the splendor the King has pledged to share with his children.

But we have been called to more.

We are also citizens of the Kingdom and subjects of the King. In every facet of our lives (because Christ is Lord of all) we have been called to live in a manner "worthy of the Kingdom of God."[4] We rejoice in his reign. We revel in his rule. We celebrate his commands. They shape our hearts. They govern our decisions. They give us our bearings in the world. They show us how to live and flourish in life.

But there is more. We have been called to be agents of the Kingdom in the world. N.T. Wright writes:

With Jesus, God's rescue operation has been put into effect once and for all. A great door has swung open in the cosmos which can never again be shut. It's the door to the prison where we've been kept chained up. We are offered freedom: freedom to experience God's rescue of ourselves, to go through the open door and explore the new world to which we now have access. In particular, *we are all invited—summoned, actually—to discover, through following Jesus, that this new world is indeed a place of justice, spirituality, relationship, and beauty, and that we are not only to enjoy it as such but to work at bringing it to birth on earth as in heaven.*[5]

We have been summoned.

TREACHERY IN THE KINGDOM

Contentment is a virtue. Complacency is not. Contentment is an acceptance of our situation in life with a thankful, trusting heart, believing that all things come to us through the hands of a loving heavenly Father. Complacency is acquiescing in a status quo that deviates from God's desires. It is an unwillingness to put anything at risk in order to bring a change in conditions that we know are wrong before God.

In the 1970's Francis Schaeffer warned that the United States, on the heels of its European forebears, had entered a post-Christian era. Values and convictions that once held our culture together no longer did. All that remained of Christianity for many were memories without power, words without meaning, and rituals without reality.[6] He saw frightening portents of what might lie ahead and sounded a prophetic alarm. What he saw, to his dismay, was that many who bore the name of Christ had slowly, quietly, and uncritically come to embrace cultural values that were seriously at odds with Christ and his ways. Chief among them were personal peace and affluence.[7]

They were dressed (disguised) in religious garb to gain acceptance in the Church, and treated as if there were a God-given right to them.

This is still the heart of our complacency. Personal peace and affluence are the premium values of too many who profess faith in Christ. Here is the truth: They are the little patch of turf people protect because it is all that is left to them in a pitiful existence. They are attractive prospects only for a shrunken life that is not worth living. Worse than that, treasuring them and organizing our lives around them is treachery in the Kingdom. It is a betrayal of the King. We become the traitors.

It doesn't have to be this way. If you find yourself here, wake up! Rouse yourself from this fatal trance! Christ calls you! His Kingdom summons you! It is the only hope for our world! It is the only cause worth living and dying for! If your heart is filled and satisfied with God, and your life is given to a quest for righteousness, peace, and joy, comfort and wealth will have no appeal to you. In the Kingdom of God you are offered something far greater: the investment of a life and the adventure of a lifetime.

THE TRANSFORMATION OF KINGDOM AGENTS

For righteousness, peace, and joy to transform the world *through* us they must first be true *of* us. If we are not shaped by them, they will never shape the world. The world has seen too little of these life-traits in those who profess faith in Christ. For many, the first things that come to mind are dogmatism, judgmentalism, and hypocrisy, and, on a larger scale, crusades, inquisitions, and colonialism. Whether their appraisal is entirely fair or not, it is a great tragedy that too many have done too little to make the world a better place, and too many, in the name of Christ (but not in the way of Christ), have subverted the true aims and ways of the Kingdom.

By now you can see that we are not within shouting distance of a self-absorbed pursuit of joy that ignores, and isolates itself from, the suffering of our fallen, broken world. This is simply not the kind of joy God offers. He doesn't offer it because it would not be true to his own joy. The gifts of God are always true reflections of the Giver.

If we think of the righteousness, peace, and joy of God's Kingdom as somehow distinct from God himself, it can only be because we are thinking of earthly kings and kingdoms, where a kingdom is a realm that is distinct from its king, and kings come and go while the kingdom remains. But this is not true of the Kingdom of God. The Kingdom of God is a descriptive way of referring to God himself in his sovereign and active reign over human affairs. To say that the Kingdom of God is righteousness, peace, and joy, is to say that these things characterize God's heart, his desires for humanity, and his commitment to bring these things about. They become ours when we harmonize our hearts with God's, tune our wills to his, and align our life-purpose with his purposes. Righteousness, peace, and joy in the Holy Spirit are the answer to our prayer for God's Kingdom to come and his will to be done on earth as it is in heaven.

You can be an activist without this. You might even adopt causes that are compatible with the Kingdom of God. But you can't be an activist for the Kingdom without harmonizing your heart with God's, tuning your will to his, and aligning your life-purpose with his plans for the world. Kingdom activists are people after God's own heart.[8] They love what God loves and hate what he hates. Jesus himself provides the paradigm:

Of the Son he says . . .

> "You have loved righteousness and hated wickedness;
> therefore God, your God, has anointed you
>   with the oil of gladness beyond your companions." (Hebrews 1:8-9)

Loving righteousness (as God does) and hating wickedness (as God does) are the north and south poles of Kingdom activism. They are the axis that orients all that we do. We embrace and promote all that is good, and we seek to overcome all that is evil (by promoting all that is good.)[9] Our incentive is that if we stay close to the heart of God, we will know the same extravagant, God-given gladness that strengthened and sustained Jesus in all that he did.

KINGDOM MOTIVATION

Paul wrote to the church at Rome, "Rejoice with those who rejoice; weep with those who weep."[10] Only those who can weep can also rejoice.[11] Sorrow and joy are drawn from the same emotional well. Think of emotions as concerned ways of interpreting and responding to the world.[12] To say that emotions are concerned means that they have something invested in the world. The way things are, and the way things ought to be, matter. When something has gone wrong, the joyful heart weeps, even if, in a larger frame of reference, it sees reasons for joy.

Sorrow and joy are both dimensions of love.[13] To say that God loves the world is to say that he affirms and rejoices in his handiwork, is saddened by our sin, and laments our suffering. He is not the God of Deists, who has removed himself from the world and looks on in transcendent disinterest. He has bound himself to his creation in covenant love. He is passionately interested and actively involved – so much so that he became one of us in Christ. And so it must be for his people, if we seek to love as God does. The Christian path of joy is not the Stoic path of resignation and apathy. It is a life of passion and costly involvement. It ventures everything for joy and risks sorrow in the quest.

If you open your heart to joy you cannot close it to sorrow. If you delight in justice, as God does,[14] your heart will be broken by injustice in the world. If you love mercy,[15] you will be devastated by the world's cruelty. If you rejoice in the beauty and wonder of God's handiwork, you can only mourn the ways in which it is despoiled. If it is a pleasure for you when God is honored, you must also embrace the anguish of seeing him dishonored. If you find your joy in the glory of God, you can only be dismayed when others ignore him, treat him irreverently, scorn him or regard him with disdain. Jesus taught his followers, "Blessed are those who mourn."[16] Even if there is beatitude in our lamentation, we must still lament, because we take seriously the evil in our world. Paul understood this well when he characterized his own experience as "sorrowful, yet always rejoicing."[17] In our world, sorrow and joy are often soul mates. They are traveling companions on the path of life.

Joy will stir your heart. It will awaken slumbering affections. It will arouse suppressed and forgotten emotions. It will move you deeply, not only to feel, but to act. You will "rejoice with those who rejoice" and "weep with those who weep."[18] You will be compelled to join others in their joy, or give yourself to those who sorrow for the sake of their joy. You will not be able to sit on your hands: You will raise them in praise, or lend them to help. It is not possible to be joyful and do otherwise. James Gilman is right: "Indeed, joy is a primary emotional force without which love's project of sorrowing with the poor [or any project of the Kingdom], is unlikely to be accomplished."[19]

When sorrow and joy meet in the same heart at the same time, compassion is the result. We grieve the pain of another and find ourselves inspired to do something: not as a duty but a delight, not as a sacrifice, but as a celebration of God's love moving through us to those who are in need. We have no sense of loss, only gain. Our joy is greater because of what we do, and even greater because we see Jesus in it: ". . . looking to Jesus, the author and perfecter of our faith, who *for the joy that was set before him* endured the cross, despising the shame, and is seated at the right hand of the throne of God."[20]

Let your heart break with his over sin and its devastating results in our world. Let it become your pain. Your sorrow. And then let his joy become yours. Let it motivate you, inspire you, and empower you to do whatever he calls you to do for the sake of his Kingdom.

Although it can easily become sinister, there are times when anger is the right response to evil and its wreckage in our world. Who can forget the story of Jesus in the temple, overturning tables and driving out money mongers who exploited the poor and perverted God's intent for that sacred place?[21] There are times when sorrow is a suitable response. Jesus also wept.[22] He taught that those who mourn sin and its devastating outcomes are blessed.[23]

Anger's life is too brief and unpredictable; sorrow's strength, too small. It is joy that moves us beyond anger and sorrow to costly and constructive action in the world. Jesus-followers in first century Macedonia left us an example:

> We want you to know, brothers, about the grace of God that has been given among the churches of Macedonia, for in a severe test of affliction, *their abundance of joy* and their extreme poverty have overflowed in a wealth of generosity on their part. For they gave according to their means, as I can testify, and beyond their means, of their own accord, begging us earnestly for the favor of taking part in the relief of the saints – and this, not as we expected, but they gave themselves first to the Lord and then by the will of God to us. (2 Corinthians 8:1-5)

Hearts on fire for the Kingdom are ablaze with joy. It is unquenchable. Irrepressible. Uncontainable. It knows no cost too great. No deed too demeaning. No task too troublesome. There is joy in all of it.

QUESTIONS FOR THOUGHT AND DISCUSSION

1. Talk about the calling of Christians to be agents of the Kingdom, as opposed to merely being citizens of the Kingdom.

2. How do you see personal peace and affluence playing out in Christian circles with which you are familiar? In your own life? How can life in and for the Kingdom change this?

3. Discuss this quote:

   > For righteousness, peace, and joy to transform the world *through* us they must first be true *of* us. If we are not shaped by them, they will never shape the world. The world has seen too little of these life-traits in those who profess faith in Christ. Too often the first things that come to the minds of those who look at Christianity from the outside are dogmatism, judgmentalism, and hypocrisy, and those who think in the larger terms of Christendom think of crusades, inquisitions and colonialism.

4. Discuss the relationship between sorrow and joy in your life. How can you cultivate both in the way you respond to the world around you?

5. Read 2 Corinthians 8:1-5 and explore the role of joy in the sacrificial giving of the church in Corinth. How does this inspire you?

CHAPTER 5

KINGDOM ADVENTURES

KINGDOM VISION

W e can see much that is wrong in the world with our eyes. Seeing possibilities for righteousness, peace, and joy in tangible situations requires spiritual vision.[1] Os Guinness has written:

> Faith's task is to join hands with the past and future to hold down God's will in the present. The present moment is the disputed territory for faith, a no-man's land between past and future, ground either to be seized by obedience or lost to disobedience. Visionary faith stakes out its possession of land and does so with energy and enthusiasm that comes from its knowledge of what the reclaimed land will one day be.[2]

Visionary faith is a creative force in the world: seeing what is not, but might be, and then seeking to bring it about. The creativity of visionary faith comes in many shapes and sizes, because it is sourced in an infinitely imaginative God: Envisioning a cure for a disease, finding work for an unemployed neighbor, discovering a solution for drought or blighted crops, microfinancing business and employment opportunities in developing countries, seeing the possibilities that might come from mentoring a boy without a father or a girl without a mother, dreaming of homes and families for orphans. No two visionaries will see the same thing, and that is a good thing! God inspires us differently and then puts us in different places because he knows that the vision he inspires within us, consecrated to him, will further his Kingdom in ways that are unique to us. Joy illumines our vision of life. Because it connects us with God and his Kingdom at work, joy enables us to see what others cannot, and empowers us to do what others dare not.

QUESTS FOR THE KINGDOM

I love this conversation between Frodo Baggins and Sam Gamgee in Peter Jackson's *The Lord of the Rings: Two Towers,* the cinematic version of J.R.R. Tolkien's literary masterpiece. The two are hungry, exhausted, and daunted by the task they have been given to destroy the ring of power in the fires of Mordor:

Frodo: I can't do this, Sam.

Sam: I know. It's all wrong. By rights we shouldn't even be here. But we are. It's like in the great stories, Mr. Frodo. The ones that really mattered. Full of darkness and danger, they were. And sometimes you didn't want to know the end. Because how could the end be happy? How could the world go back to the way it was when so much bad had happened? But in the end, it's only a passing thing, this shadow. Even darkness must pass. A new day will come. And when the sun shines it will shine out the clearer. Those were the stories that stayed with you. That meant something, even if you were too small to understand why. But I think, Mr. Frodo, I do understand. I know now. Folk in those stories had lots of chances of turning back, only they didn't. They kept going. Because they were holding on to something.

Frodo: What are we holding onto, Sam?

Sam: That there's some good in this world, Mr. Frodo, and it's worth fighting for."

As agents of the Kingdom, we don't fight for remnants of good in our world so much as we fight for the good that the Kingdom can bring into the world. And that is worth fighting for! It is worth the danger, risks, and sacrifices we make to be part of what God is doing to bring about his rightful reign on the earth. There is no greater opportunity for heroic faith, with life-changing, world-changing results, than you will find in Kingdom adventures.

Adventures are glamorous only in Hollywood. The truth is that there is no adventure without risk, and no risk without the real possibility of failure. If you fight, you might lose. If you speak, you might not persuade. If you try, you might fail. If you love, you might not be loved in return. Kingdom agents embrace these risks and march onto the field of combat, with enemy battlements in view, for the sake of greater possibilities for the Kingdom. The Kingdom of God will not fail. It cannot, because our King is almighty. But we are not, and our actions for the Kingdom might not succeed. The war will surely be won, but battles may be lost. It might be one in which you are engaged. Kingdom agents count the cost, consider the peril, and then set out on quests for the Kingdom.

KINGDOM COURAGE

Madeleine L'Engle said that we must be "braver than we think we can be, because God is constantly calling us to be more than we are."[3] And he is constantly calling us to do things we can't do. It's no good complaining about this. It is God's way. If we give ourselves to the Kingdom, the challenges we face will be greater than we are, the obstacles bigger, and the dangers more harrowing than our hearts can bear. It isn't possible to live for the Kingdom without coming to terms with this. If we allow our weakness and fear to win, opportunities will be lost. Like vapor on a hot day, possibilities will disappear, never to come again.

Listen to the way the apostle Paul described his time in the city of Corinth: "I was with you in weakness and in fear and much trembling, and my speech and my message were not in plausible words of wisdom, but in demonstration of the Spirit and power."[4] His experience was weakness, fear, and trembling. But he refused to let these emotional forces stop him. With trembling knees, he stepped through his weakness and fear into an experience of God's power at work in and through him. That is what Kingdom courage looks like, and it turned the ancient world upside down.[5]

Where do we find courage for the Kingdom? In the overflow of joy. Joyful people are courageous because joy is more powerful than fear. Fear is weakness overwhelming our hearts; joy is God's power filling them. Nehemiah knew this when he encouraged a disheartened nation: "The joy of the LORD is your strength!"[6] Godly women of old knew this: "Strength and dignity are her clothing, and she laughs at the time to come."[7] Joy will empower you to walk through your fears into adventurous living for the Kingdom.[8] You might be able to screw up your courage in other ways, but why would you when joy is offered?

SUFFERING FOR THE KINGDOM

We must be courageous, because we may suffer for the Kingdom. Many around the world do. Read these words of the ancient Seer, and put yourself into the last sentence:

49

> And I heard a loud voice in heaven, saying, "Now the salvation and the power and the kingdom of our God and the authority of his Christ have come, for the accuser of our brothers has been thrown down, who accuses them day and night before our God. And they have conquered him by the blood of the Lamb and by the word of their testimony, for *they loved not their lives even unto death.* (Revelation 12:10-11)

The clash of kingdoms may take place in the invisible, intangible realm, but it plays out in the visible, tangible world. It may impact our physical well-being. Our freedom. Our finances. Our family. It may come with words, but it may also come with fists and flames of fire. In time, it may come with bullets and bombs. The skies may be filled with them. Streets may flow with their bloody devastation. Jesus and his earliest followers knew well the prospects of suffering, but they also knew that joy would see them through.[9]

Christians through the centuries have faced death for embracing Christ. They knew what lay before them, and mocked it with an undaunted and a defiant joy. Let me tell you a few stories.

Ignatius, a disciple of the apostle John was executed just after the turn of the first century. As he was being arrested it was said of him that he "joyfully submitted his limbs to the fetters," and when he was told that he would be fed to the lions, he responded, "I have joy of the beasts that are prepared for me!"[10]

A few decades later another disciple of John, Polycarp, was arrested for his faith in Christ. When threatened with the pyre, he responded, "Why do you delay? Bring against me what you please." A witness reported that as he spoke "he appeared in a transport of joy and confidence, and his countenance shown with a certain heavenly grace."[11]

With these two men the last link to the eyewitnesses of Christ came to an end, but the heritage of courageous joy lived on. According to Ambrose, St. Agnes was beheaded in A.D. 304 under the persecution of the Roman emperor, Diocletian. Upon learning that this was to be her fate, Agnes was "filled with joy on hearing this sentence, [and] went to the place of execution more cheerfully than others go to their wedding."[12]

A contemporary of hers, Vincent of Saragossa, was tortured for refusing to recant his faith in Christ. He endured the rack, iron hooks tearing into his flesh, salt rubbed into his wounds and finally a gridiron of fire and spikes. Augustine wrote that "the more Vincent suffered, the greater seemed to be the inward joy and consolation of his soul."[13]

John Huss, the early reformer, met the same kind of fate with the same courageous joy. With hands manacled behind his back, his neck bound to the stake by a chain, and straw and wood heaped up to his chin, Huss refused to recant his understanding of the Gospel. Instead, he exclaimed to his executioners, "I shall die with joy today in the faith of the Gospel which I have preached."[14]

If we should face death for Jesus, will we face it down with joy?

SHOULDER TO SHOULDER FOR THE KINGDOM

Courage may call you to set out on a path alone, but wisdom will look to see if God has put the same quest in the hearts of others. Likely he has. It may be a small band, but if I read the Bible rightly, God loves starting with small things to bring great things about. It is his way. It is the way of the Kingdom. One is better than none, but two are better than one.[15] Even if they are few, there is greater strength, greater wisdom, greater resources when sisters and brothers in Christ work together to make a difference for the Kingdom.

Start by looking for allies. Fellow citizens of the Kingdom. Fellow followers of Christ. Begin the search in your local congregation.[16] You may discover embers that must be fanned into flame, and your joy will be the blaze that ignites them. Find others and take the yoke of Christ together. Set out on a quest for the Kingdom together. What you do for the Kingdom will be the best thing that could happen to your church! As people watch you step out of the dull routines of an unchallenged, unspent life into adventures for the Kingdom, many will be inspired to join you.

You will also find allies beyond your local congregation, in the city or town where you live. Christ has people in surprising places whose hearts yearn for something bigger and better to live for.[17] They may be in other churches or Christian organizations. They may not yet understand the restlessness in their souls or the longing in their hearts, but when you speak with them about investing their life for the Kingdom they will recognize you as the one they have been waiting for, and the Kingdom of God as the one thing worth giving their lives for. They are out there. They may even be looking for you!

There are also *co-belligerents* for the Kingdom.[18] Their interests and concerns overlap with yours, but they don't see their action as service for the Kingdom. They may be inspired by Jesus, or they may feel compelled to act on humanitarian grounds. To use the words of Jesus, they are "not far from the Kingdom."[19] They may not be in it yet, but they have drawn near. Like the scribe of whom Jesus spoke, their values and life-commitments are commendable, even if they haven't yet embraced him as Lord of all. It is often the case that a passion for justice and acts of compassion are evidence of God's grace at work, and of hearts that have been touched by him. Join God in what he is seeking to do in their lives, and join them in the good they are seeking to do in the world.

I would cast my net broadly in looking for others who can help advance the cause of the Kingdom. The apostle Paul led a campaign to collect contributions for Jews who had fallen victim to drought in Palestine.[20] He focused on Christian communities in his search for help, but do you think he would have turned away a generous contribution from a God-fearing Gentile who was not yet a follower of Jesus? I don't! If he had had the opportunity to speak with the emperor of Rome and ask him to relieve the tax burden on poor Jews in Palestine, do you think he would have? I do! It is here that we should listen to the words of Jesus: "He who is not against me is for me."[21] The Spirit of God is at work in ways and places and people that we would never guess. Agents of the Kingdom love being surprised by him, and move with the currents of his activity wherever they find them.[22]

STAYING ON COURSE FOR THE KINGDOM

Anything worthwhile requires the investment of a lifetime. Anything that lasts requires the commitment of several generations. This runs against the grain of our culture and its desire for quick results. The Kingdom of God is not ours to build or to expand, to use popular idioms. That is God's work, and it is not limited to our lifespans. If anyone has the *big picture* and the *long view* of history, it is he.

It is ours to live in the Kingdom, to live under the rule of our King, and to be ready as agents of the Kingdom whenever we are summoned. It is ours to be faithful, fully invested, fully engaged, steadfast, patient, and persevering for as long as God gives us breath. I hope it will be decades for you if Christ does not come to bring his Kingdom in its fullness. However long or short our journey may be, there is encouragement in the words of the apostle:

> Therefore, my beloved brothers, be steadfast, immovable, always abounding in the work of the Lord, knowing that in the Lord your labor is not in vain. (1 Corinthians 15:58)

> Do not be deceived: God is not mocked, for whatever one sows, that will he also reap. For the one who sows to his own flesh will from the flesh reap corruption, but the one who sows to the Spirit will from the Spirit reap eternal life. And let us not grow weary of doing good, for in due season we will reap, if we do not give up. (Galatians 6:8-9)

QUESTIONS FOR THOUGHT AND DISCUSSION

1. How can you develop visionary faith and encourage it in others in your Christian circles?

2. Discuss this quote:

> Adventures are glamorous only in Hollywood. The truth is that there is no adventure without risk, and no risk without the real possibility of failure. If you fight, you might lose. If you speak, you might not persuade. If you try, you might fail. If you love, you might not be loved in return. Kingdom agents embrace these risks and march onto the field of combat, with enemy battlements in view, for the sake of greater possibilities for the Kingdom.

3. Discuss this quote:

> Madeleine L'Engle said that we must be "braver than we think we can be, because God is constantly calling us to be more than we are." And he is constantly calling us to do things we can't do. It's no good complaining about this. It is God's way.

4. Talk about the persecution of Christians around the world today. How can you pray for them more consistently and prepare for the possibility of suffering yourself?

5. Can you identify potential allies and co-belligerents for the Kingdom in your network of relationships? What Kingdom projects can you enlist them in?

CHAPTER 6

LIVING IN THE KINGDOM

SURRENDER AND THE KINGDOM

I f you ask God to bring his Kingdom to your heart, and to do his will in your life as it is done in heaven, how do you give yourself to this prayer? If I could suggest one word to you, it would be *surrender*. It is about saying "No" to ourselves in order to say "Yes" to God. We see this in the One whose life perfectly embodied the Kingdom of God. His closest disciples never forgot his prayer: "Not my will, but yours be done."[1] This was not an isolated petition in a moment of crisis. It resounded with every beat of his heart. It was carried on every breath until the last breath rattled in his lungs and escaped with the words, "It is finished."[2]

It is often the case that our "Yes" to one thing implies a "No" to other things. If I say that I will spend the afternoon at my son's baseball game, I can't be in the mountains on a hike or at home mowing the lawn at the same time. This kind of "No" is part of our finitude. The "No" involved in our surrender to God is much deeper. This "No" is a relinquishing. A renunciation. An abdication. An abandonment of everything to the reign of God. A disposing of all things in order to put ourselves fully at his disposal.

This is what Jesus had in mind for us when he said, "If any one would come after me, let him deny himself, take up his cross, and follow me."[3] There must be a "No" to ourselves, a death to ourselves, before there can be a

"Yes" to Christ and new life in him. This is the way the apostle Paul approached life:

> I have been crucified with Christ. It is no longer I who live, but Christ who lives in me. And the life I now live in the flesh I live by faith in the Son of God, who loved me and gave himself for me. (Galatians 2:20)

> But whatever gain I had, I counted as loss for the sake of Christ. Indeed, I count everything as loss because of the surpassing worth of knowing Christ Jesus my Lord. For his sake I have suffered the loss of all things and count them as rubbish, in order that I may gain Christ. (Philippians 3:7-9)

The things we count as loss are the things we surrender for the Kingdom. We must say "No" to everything else in order to say "Yes" to Christ. At its innermost, however, this is not about things. It is about us. It is about surrendering ourselves to God: "I appeal to you therefore, brothers, by the mercies of God, to present your bodies as a living sacrifice, holy and acceptable to God, which is your spiritual worship."[4]

We are called to embrace a radical change in orientation, from living for ourselves to living for Christ: "For the love of Christ controls us, because we have concluded this: that one has died for all, therefore all have died; and he died for all, that those who live might no longer live for themselves but for him who for their sake died and was raised."[5]

Living for ourselves can play out in two ways: self-promotion and self-protection. We can't promote ourselves and the Kingdom at the same time. If our orientation in life is advancing our own position, power, prestige, or possessions, the Kingdom of God will not advance through us. By the very nature of things, it cannot. It is also the case that if our energy is spent protecting ourselves and our interests, the Kingdom will not be furthered through us. It cannot.

Self-promotion is more evident than self-protection. Self-promotion is obvious because it seeks to impress. Self-protection is subtle and insidious because it often involves things we don't do. We don't do things that put our interests at risk. We keep our activities safe. We cocoon ourselves from potential danger. Self-promotion and self-protection are both self-centered ways of living. Both disqualify us from being agents for the Kingdom. The only remedy is self-surrender, and a heart that considers it joy to do so.

The surrender required by the Kingdom goes to the deepest part of who we are and to the most practical dimensions of our lives. It touches our possessions. Jesus said, "You cannot serve God and money."[6] If we hold tightly to things that money buys (material goods or a sense of safety and security for our future) we bow to this false god. If we accumulate and hoard, we are not merely devotees but slaves. The power of money is broken and we are liberated from its shackles when we surrender our possessions to God and joyfully give to others. (The only things we should have in this world are the things God loans back to us after we have surrendered everything to him.) It is then, in the words of Jesus, that we "enter the Kingdom of God."[7]

Surrender includes our time. Kingdom calls are rarely convenient. Sometimes they are an emergency. Sometimes they require a change of plans for an evening or a weekend. Often we must let go of what we had arranged to do in order to embrace what God wants us to do and his Kingdom needs us to do.

What about the way we spend our holidays? Sometimes the best Thanksgiving Day will be serving food to the homeless in our community. The best Christmas season may include volunteering time to give gifts to the poor, to orphans, to those who are home-bound, or to children with a parent in prison.

Surrendering our time will influence what we do with our vacations. God has designed respites as important beats in the rhythm of life, but there are also times when the best break from work is helping people who are not in a position to help themselves (Jesus himself left us the example of doing works of compassion on the Sabbath.) The best family times may not involve a vacation destination, but a family project that devotes time and resources to others in need.

What about retirement? You can withdraw from the workforce, but there is no retirement from the Kingdom. In fact your retirement years could be the most spiritually productive and fruitful time of your life. But you must hold your time with a loose grip. It must be included in your surrender for the Kingdom.

Surrender for the Kingdom includes hearth and home. Jesus is not a stay-at-home-Savior! His heart is for the world. All nations. All peoples. And that means that his followers must venture from their homes to be his emissaries. It was not unintentional that Jesus put "house" in the first place of things we must be prepared to leave for his sake.[8] This is not about moving to increase the value of your real estate investments, or moving for the sake of a job, though God may lead you to do both. It is about embracing the possibility of leaving your house behind and going to another place because God calls you to do it for his Kingdom. Because there are opportunities for Kingdom service somewhere else.

Surrender for the Kingdom includes our relationships. This is not about bonds of love. We should do everything we can to strengthen them. It is not about abandoning God-given responsibilities in marriage and family. However, Jesus clearly envisioned the possibility of leaving "father, mother, sister, brother" for his sake.[9] Treasured relationships often involve close proximity, and that is good. But there are times when we must let go of a lesser good for the sake of a greater good. Serving the Kingdom may require us to venture to places far from those we love.

Are you open to these things? This side of your decision to surrender may involve painful deliberation. On the other side you will find a joy so great that you will scold yourself for not making the decision sooner!

FRUITFULNESS FOR THE KINGDOM

We are not called to build the Kingdom of God or to advance the Kingdom. Only God can do these things. It is ours to seek the Kingdom, pray for it, live in it, and act on its behalf. In a confrontation with religious leaders in Jerusalem, Jesus said, "The kingdom of God will be taken away from you and given to a people producing its fruits."[10] God holds us responsible for being fruitful for his Kingdom.

Fruitfulness for the Kingdom happens when it is a way of living, wherever you are and whatever you do. It requires a radical openness to Christ. There will be times when he calls you to act, not because you are uniquely gifted to do it, but because you are the only one there to do it. The opportunity for the Kingdom will be lost unless you seize it. Fruit for the Kingdom will be produced through your obedience in the moment. You may step forward in weakness, fear, and trembling, but your obedience will put you in a position to see God's power at work through you.[11] Don't close your heart to the special circumstances God puts in your life. Don't wait for someone else to come along. It is your moment. Your opportunity. Your call to obedience. Your opportunity for Kingdom fruitfulness. Your opportunity for greater joy.

As you think about being fruitful for the Kingdom, start with those who are closest to you, in the community of faith, and then work outward. Paul wrote, "So then, as we have opportunity, let us do good to all, but especially to those of the household of faith." [12]   This is what makes Christian communities vibrant, winsome, and attractive to those who are on the outside looking in. Others will be drawn to you (plural) and that, in turn, will create new opportunities and an expanding circle of influence and fruitfulness for the Kingdom.

If we could see fruitfulness for the Kingdom as God does, we would see millions of acts around the world every day: almost all of them quiet and humble; most, small enough that no one but the recipient would notice. The media will never report them, but they are headlines in heaven. Some may require planning, training, and skills dedicated to the Kingdom, but most will involve daily, intentional, situational obedience to Christ. They make a difference in the lives of those who encounter Kingdom activists. Together they will make a difference in our world.

LIVING WITH A FULL AND JOYFUL HEART

Many of us are accustomed to what I call *duty-and-guilt* motivational pitches: "You have a duty to do this, and you should feel guilty if you don't!" Not many actually say this, but their intent is clear. For some church leaders it is a polished art. For some parents, too, and for some well-meaning family members and friends. This only burdens people with guilt-feelings if they don't say "Yes," and makes them dismal in their duty if they do. How attractive is that? How winsome to the world will that be?

Duty is the wrong place to find our motivation. So are the needs we see around us. One of the things I was taught early in my life of discipleship (a father's words of wisdom to his son) is that *a need does not constitute a call.* There are too many needs in our world. We are not called to meet them all. The commands of Jesus constitute a call, because we are summoned to obedience. Our gifting constitutes a call, because we are charged with being responsible stewards.   But needs alone do not imply a call.   There were many who needed healing whom Jesus did not heal. There were many hungry whom he did not feed. There were many who lived in poverty who were not relieved by his alms.[13] There were many who were oppressed by Rome, but Jesus did not marshal his time and resources for that cause. He did only those things that he knew his Father was calling him to do.[14] He met needs, but he was not governed by them.

What should motivate and guide us in the choices we make for the Kingdom? The best place to begin is not guilt laid upon us, or the needs we see around us, but the gifts, talents, delights, and desires God places within us: "For we are his workmanship, created in Christ Jesus for good works, which God prepared beforehand, that we should walk in them."[15] We are God's workmanship. The good deeds he has prepared for us are an outward expression of his handiwork in us. This means that when we start thinking about how to invest our time, treasures, and talents for the Kingdom, we should look at how we have been crafted and shaped by God. What strengths has he given us? What special gifting and talents do we bring to the Kingdom? What are the dreams and desires that stir our souls? What makes us fully and joyfully alive as we venture into the world for the Kingdom? A Gideon's band of three hundred with joyful, adventurous hearts will make a much greater impact for the Kingdom than tens of thousands who would rather stay at home, and who respond only to the pressure of duty and guilt.

Joy is the strongest motivation for investing your life for the Kingdom. It took me three volumes (*Path of Life* and *Rivers of Delight, Volumes 1 and 2*) to describe what I believe living with a full and joyful heart looks like (which – though you may doubt it – says more about joy than it does my wordiness). Rather than review, I urge you to listen to joy's call. It was powerful enough to motivate Jesus to endure the Cross for you. His joy beckons you. The joy of the Kingdom awaits you. Give yourself fully to it, and make it a way of life to:

➢ Look for opportunities to do righteousness and do it.

➢ Look for openness to peace and broker it.

➢ Look for receptivity to joy and cultivate it.

➢ Look for faith and stir it.

➢ Look for hope and share it.

➢ Look for love and celebrate it.

➢ Look for goodness and commend it.

➢ Look for beauty and appreciate it.

➢ Look for truth and affirm it.

➢ Look for excellence and extol it.

➢ Look for achievement and applaud it.

➢ Look for honesty and honor it.

➢ Look for diligence and praise it.

➢ Look for industry and congratulate it.

➢ Look for courage and cheer it.

➢ Look for generosity and enlarge it.

Living in the Kingdom

- ➢ Look for a wrong and right it.

- ➢ Look for injustice and challenge it.

- ➢ Look for evil and overcome it.

- ➢ Look for sin and confront it.

- ➢ Look for darkness and expose it.

- ➢ Look for error and correct it.

- ➢ Look for indolence and dare it.

- ➢ Look for apathy and question it.

- ➢ Look for complacency and rouse it.

- ➢ Look for wastefulness and reprove it.

- ➢ Look for a need and meet it.

- ➢ Look for a problem and solve it.

- ➢ Look for an obstacle and surmount it.

- ➢ Look for the plain and adorn it.

- ➢ Look for strife and end it.

- ➢ Look for hostility and resolve it.

➤ Look for discord and bring harmony to it.

➤ Look for the unskilled and teach them.

➤ Look for the lost and guide them.

➤ Look for the weak and empower them.

➤ Look for the destitute and deliver them.

➤ Look for victims and rescue them.

➤ Look for the persecuted and protect them.

➤ Look for the oppressed and advocate for them.

➤ Look for the voiceless and speak for them.

➤ Look for the disabled and help them.

➤ Look for the lonely and befriend them.

➤ Look for the fearful and embolden them.

➤ Look for the disheartened and encourage them.

➤ Look for the brokenhearted and comfort them.

➤ Look for the sorrowful and weep with them.

➤ Look for the grieving and console them.

LIVING IN THE KINGDOM

- ➤ Look for the suffering and show kindness to them.

- ➤ Look for the hopeless and inspire them.

- ➤ Look for the sick and care for them.

- ➤ Look for the poor and provide for them.

- ➤ Look for the disadvantaged and train them.

- ➤ Look for the hungry and feed them.

- ➤ Look for the homeless and shelter them.

- ➤ Look for widows and support them.

- ➤ Look for the elderly and respect them.

- ➤ Look for single parents and relieve them.

- ➤ Look for the fatherless and mentor them.

- ➤ Look for the motherless and nurture them.

- ➤ Look for the orphaned and adopt them.

- ➤ Look for prisoners and visit them.

- ➤ Look for enemies and reconcile them.

- ➤ Look for the unlovely and love them.

KINGDOM MANIFESTO

➤ Look for the forgotten and remember them.

➤ Look for outcasts and include them.

➤ Look for resources and steward them.

➤ Look for open hearts and open doors and resource them.

➤ In every possible way, proclaim the Gospel of the Kingdom to a world that desperately needs it!

QUESTIONS FOR THOUGHT AND DISCUSSION

1. What is the difference between self-promotion and self-protection, and how do you see them playing out in your life?

2. After reading this chapter, are you aware of areas of your life that you need to surrender for the sake of the Kingdom? What makes it so hard to do this?

3. Discuss this quote and what it might look like in your life:

   > Fruitfulness for the Kingdom happens when it is a way of living in the world, wherever you are and whatever you do. It involves radical openness to Christ. There will be times when he calls you to act, not because you are uniquely gifted to do it, but because you are the only one there to do it. The opportunity for the Kingdom will be lost unless you seize it.

4. Have you experienced "duty-and-guilt" motivational pitches? How do you typically respond to them? Do you find yourself using them with others? How is joy a more powerful motivator?

5. Read Ephesians 2:10 and talk about how the good works that God has for you are related to who you are as his unique workmanship.

ABOUT THE AUTHOR

In 1983 Rick and Sue Howe moved to Boulder, Colorado, where they raised three children – Amberle, Lorien, and Jamison – and have devoted more than thirty years to campus ministry at the University of Colorado. In addition to writing and speaking, Rick now leads University Ministries, whose mission is to "inspire and nurture a thoughtful pursuit of Christ, one student, one professor, one university at a time." To learn more about Rick, visit his website at www.rickhowe.org. You can also follow him on Facebook at *Rick Howe on Joy* and on Twitter @rickhoweonjoy. To learn more about University Ministries, see www.university-ministries.org.

ENDNOTES

INTRODUCTION

[1] The observation of C.S. Lewis is significant here:

> If you read history you will find that the Christians that did most for the present world were those who thought most of the next. The apostles themselves, who set out on foot to convert the Roman Empire, the great men who built up the Middle Ages, the English evangelicals who abolished the slave trade, all left their mark on earth, precisely because their minds were occupied with heaven. It is since Christians have largely ceased to think of the other world that they have become so ineffective in this one. Aim at heaven and you will get earth "thrown in." Aim at earth and you will get neither.

C.S. Lewis, *Mere Christianity* (New York: Simon & Schuster, 1996), p. 119.

Earthly-minded Christians in our day merely reflect the world. Christopher Lasch put it this way:

> After the political turmoil of the sixties, Americans have retreated to purely personal preoccupations. Having no hope of improving their lives in any of the ways that matter, people have convinced themselves that what matters is psychic self-improvement: getting in touch with their feelings, eating health food, taking lessons in ballet or belly-dancing, immersing themselves in the wisdom of the East, jogging, learning how to "relate," overcoming the "fear of pleasure."
>
> The contemporary climate is therapeutic, not religious. People today hunger not for personal satisfaction, let alone for the restoration of an earlier age, but for the feeling, the momentary illusion, of personal well-being, health and psychic security.

Christopher Lasch, *The Culture of Narcissism* (New York: Norton, 1978), pp. 4, 7.

[2] Paul Tournier described the problem this way:

> What I am concerned about are the large numbers of people who are victims of a tragic misunderstanding. They take no further interest in worldly matters because their interest has – quite properly – been awakened in regard to the spiritual verities, as if the latter could exist in themselves in the abstract, outside of their incarnation in the world.

Paul Tournier, *The Adventure of Living* (New York: Harper & Row, 1976), p. 202.

[3] "In him, according to the purpose of him who accomplishes all things according to the counsel of his will." (Ephesians 1:11)

4   See:

> The sentence is by the decree of the watchers, the decision by the word of the holy
> ones, to the end that living may know that the Most High rules the kingdom of men,
> and gives it to whom he will, and sets over it the lowliest of men.' . . . that you shall be
> driven from among men, and your dwelling shall be with the beasts of the field; you
> shall be made to eat grass like an ox, and you shall be wet with the dew of heaven, and
> seven times shall pass over you, till you know that the Most High rules the kingdom of
> men, and gives it to whom he will. . . and you shall be driven from among men, and
> your dwelling shall be with the beasts of the field; and you shall be made to eat grass
> like an ox; and seven times shall pass over you, until you have learned that the Most
> High rules the kingdom of men and gives it to whom he will. (Daniel 4: 17, 25, 32)

5   "Are not two sparrows sold for a penny? And not one of them will fall to the ground
without your Father's will." (Matthew 10:29)

6   Karl Barth said that joy "should not be limited by the suffering of life, because even life's
suffering (or what we regard as such) comes from God, the very One who summons us
to rejoice." Karl Barth, *Church Dogmatics*, eds., Geoffrey W. Bromiley, T. F. Torrance
(Edinburgh: T.&T. Clark, 1968), Vol. III, Part 4, p. 383. This is so, whether you take
this in the strong sense of God's causal activity, or you see suffering related permissively
to the will of God. Either way, God takes ultimate responsibility.

7   Quoted in see William Morrice, *Joy in the New Testament* (Grand Rapids, Michigan:
Eerdmans, 1984), p. 107.

8   Matthew 5:11-12a

9   Acts 5:41

10   Colossians 1:24

11   James 1:2, ESV

12   1 Peter 4:13

13   If we ask, "Why?" when we experience or see suffering, no answer may be given. If we
ask the far more fruitful question, "To what end?" the Scriptures give us much more to
work with.

CHAPTER 1: INTRODUCTION TO THE KINGDOM

1   This part of the story is told in the second chapter, "The Shadow of the Past," following
Bilbo's birthday party and departure for Rivendell.

2   J.R.R. Tolkien, *The Fellowship of the Ring: Being the First Part of the Lord of the Rings* (Boston, New York: Houghten Mifflin Co., 1982) pp. 42-43.

3   Ibid., p. 50.

4   Matthew 6:10

5   See the following:

> How you are fallen from heaven,
> O Lucifer, son of the morning!
> How you are cut down to the ground,
> You who weakened the nations!
> For you have said in your heart:
> 'I will ascend into heaven,
> I will exalt my throne above the stars of God;
> I will also sit on the mount of the congregation
> On the farthest sides of the north;
> I will ascend above the heights of the clouds,
> I will be like the Most High.'
> Yet you shall be brought down to Sheol,
> To the lowest depths of the Pit. (Isaiah 14:12-15, NKJV)

> Then Jesus was led up by the Spirit into the wilderness to be tempted by the devil. (Matthew 4:1)

> And the tempter came and said to him, "If you are the Son of God, command these stones to become loaves of bread." (Matthew 4:3)

> Then Jesus said to him, "Away with you, Satan! For it is written, 'You shall worship the Lord your God, and Him only you shall serve.'" (Matthew 4:10)
> And the great dragon was thrown down, that ancient serpent, who is called the devil and Satan, the deceiver of the whole world—he was thrown down to the earth, and his angels were thrown down with him. (Revelation 12:9)

> And I heard a loud voice in heaven, saying, "Now the salvation and the power and the kingdom of our God and the authority of his Christ have come, for the accuser of our brothers has been thrown down, who accuses them day and night before our God. (Revelation 12:10)

> You are of your father the devil, and your will is to do your father's desires. He was a murderer from the beginning, and does not stand in the truth, because there is no truth in him. When he lies, he speaks out of his own character, for he is a liar and the father of lies. (John 8:44)

In their case the god of this world has blinded the minds of the unbelievers, to keep them from seeing the light of the gospel of the glory of Christ, who is the image of God. (2 Corinthians 4:4)

6   From Martin Luther's *A Mighty Fortress Is Our God*. Luther knew this spiritual battle well. From the day he took a stand against corruption and error in the church of his day, he lived with a death sentence hanging over his head. It was no idle threat. Others before him had been killed for challenging ecclesiastical power. He never began a day without thinking it might be his last. He hesitated to marry because he knew that he might not survive to fulfill responsibilities to a wife and children. See Roland Bainton, *Here I Stand: A Life of Martin Luther* (Peabody, MA: Hendrickson Publishers, 1977), p. 292.

Luther's actions for the Kingdom roused a perilous enemy. The enemy was not the Roman Catholic church, however, but the one who found ways to work through it at that time. I would say the same thing of the magisterial reformation and its persecution of the Anabaptists. The apostle Paul's words are true in every generation: "For we do not wrestle against flesh and blood, but against the rulers, against the authorities, against the cosmic powers over this present darkness, against the spiritual forces of evil in the heavenly places." (Ephesians 6:12)

7   Colossians 1:13

8   C.S. Lewis, "Christianity and Culture" in *Christian Reflections*, ed. Walter Hooper (Grand Rapids, MI: Eerdmans, 1995), p. 33.

9   "Truly, truly, I say to you, you will weep and lament, but the world will rejoice; you will be sorrowful, but your sorrow will turn into joy." (John 16:20)

10   "He will wipe away every tear from their eyes, and death shall be no more, neither shall there be mourning nor crying nor pain any more, for the former things have passed away." (Revelation 21:4)

11   Of course, I don't know that that will be the case. But it could be suggested in this prophetic picture of the new heavens and the new earth: "And the city has no need of sun or moon to shine on it, for the glory of God gives it light, and its lamp is the Lamb. By its light will the nations walk, and the kings of the earth will bring their glory into it, and its gates will never be shut by day—and there will be no night there." (Revelation 21:23-25)

12   We are speaking here of the eschatological kingdom, which is both present and future to us. The Old Testament also speaks of God's kingdom, which refers to God's reign over human history during the era of messianic promise. See, e.g., John Bright, *The Kingdom of God: The Biblical Concept and Its Meaning for the Church* (Nashville: Abingdon,

1953), pp. 17-186. See also Bruce K. Waltke, *Old Testament Theology: The Making of the Kingdom* (Grand Rapids, MI: Zondervan).

[13]   Matthew 6:10, ESV

[14]   Mark 1:15

[15]   See:

> The Spirit of the LORD God is upon me,
>   because the LORD has anointed me
> to bring good news to the poor;
>   he has sent me to bind up the brokenhearted,
> to proclaim liberty to the captives,
>   and the opening of the prison to those who are bound;
> to proclaim the year of the LORD's favor,
>   and the day of vengeance of our God;
>   to comfort all who mourn. (Isaiah 61:1-2)

[16]   With traditional ending.

[17]   "From that time Jesus began to preach, saying, 'Repent, for the kingdom of heaven is at hand.' . . . And he went throughout all Galilee, teaching in their synagogues and proclaiming the gospel of the kingdom and healing every disease and every affliction among the people." (Matthew 4:17, 23)

[18]   See, for example, the Sermon on the Mount:

> Blessed are the poor in spirit, for theirs is the kingdom of heaven. (Matthew 5:3)

> Blessed are those who are persecuted for righteousness' sake, for theirs is the kingdom of heaven. (Matthew 5:10)

> For I tell you, unless your righteousness exceeds that of the scribes and Pharisees, you will never enter the kingdom of heaven. (Matthew 5:20)

> Your kingdom come, your will be done, on earth as it is in heaven. (Matthew 6:10)

> For yours is the kingdom and the power and the glory, forever. Amen (Matthew 6:13)

> But seek first the kingdom of God and his righteousness, and all these things will be added to you. (Matthew 6:33)

> Not everyone who says to me, "Lord, Lord," will enter the kingdom of heaven, but the one who does the will of my Father who is in heaven. (Matthew 7:21)

19   See, for example, Jesus' parables of the Kingdom in Matthew 13.

20   See:

> And if I cast out demons by Beelzebul, by whom do your sons cast them out? Therefore they will be your judges. But if it is by the Spirit of God that I cast out demons, then the kingdom of God has come upon you. Or how can someone enter a strong man's house and plunder his goods, unless he first binds the strong man? Then indeed he may plunder his house. (Matthew 12:27-29)

21   Compare:

> But if it is by the Spirit of God that I cast out demons, then the kingdom of God has come upon you. (Matthew 12:28)

> But if it is by the finger of God that I cast out demons, then the kingdom of God has come upon you. (Luke 11:20)

22   See the following:

> And he called the twelve together and gave them power and authority over all demons and to cure diseases, and he sent them out to proclaim the kingdom of God and to heal. And he said to them, "Take nothing for your journey, no staff, nor bag, nor bread, nor money; and do not have two tunics. And whatever house you enter, stay there, and from there depart. And wherever they do not receive you, when you leave that town shake off the dust from your feet as a testimony against them." And they departed and went through the villages, preaching the gospel and healing everywhere. (Luke 9:1-6)

> After this the Lord appointed seventy-two others and sent them on ahead of him, two by two, into every town and place where he himself was about to go. And he said to them, "The harvest is plentiful, but the laborers are few. Therefore pray earnestly to the Lord of the harvest to send out laborers into his harvest. Go your way; behold, I am sending you out as lambs in the midst of wolves. Carry no moneybag, no knapsack, no sandals, and greet no one on the road. Whatever house you enter, first say, 'Peace be to this house!' And if a son of peace is there, your peace will rest upon him. But if not, it will return to you. And remain in the same house, eating and drinking what they provide, for the laborer deserves his wages. Do not go from house to house. Whenever you enter a town and they receive you, eat what is set before you. Heal the sick in it and say to them, 'The kingdom of God has come near to you.' But whenever you enter a town and they do not receive you, go into its streets and say, 'Even the dust of your town that clings to our feet we wipe off against you. Nevertheless know this, that the kingdom of God has come near.' I tell you, it will be more bearable on that day for Sodom than for that town. (Luke 10:1-12)

23   "And this gospel of the kingdom will be proclaimed throughout the whole world as a

testimony to all nations, and then the end will come." (Matthew 24:14)

24 "And I tell you, you are Peter, and on this rock I will build my church, and the gates of hell shall not prevail against it. I will give you the keys of the kingdom of heaven, and whatever you bind on earth shall be bound in heaven, and whatever you loose on earth shall be loosed in heaven." (Matthew 16:18-19)

25 "He presented himself alive to them after his suffering by many proofs, appearing to them during forty days and speaking about the kingdom of God." (Acts 1:3)

26 "For the kingdom of God is not a matter of eating and drinking but of righteousness and peace and joy in the Holy Spirit." (Romans 14:17)

27 Many passages speak of the Kingdom as yet future. See for example:

> Your kingdom come, your will be done, on earth as it is in heaven. (Matthew. 6:10)

> Then the King will say to those on his right, 'Come, you who are blessed by my Father, inherit the kingdom prepared for you from the foundation of the world. (Matthew 25:34)

> Then he left the crowds and went into the house. And his disciples came to him, saying, "Explain to us the parable of the weeds of the field." He answered, "The one who sows the good seed is the Son of Man. The field is the world, and the good seed is the sons of the kingdom. The weeds are the sons of the evil one, and the enemy who sowed them is the devil. The harvest is the end of the age, and the reapers are angels. Just as the weeds are gathered and burned with fire, so will it be at the end of the age. The Son of Man will send his angels, and they will gather out of his kingdom all causes of sin and all law-breakers, and throw them into the fiery furnace. In that place there will be weeping and gnashing of teeth. Then the righteous will shine like the sun in the kingdom of their Father. He who has ears, let him hear. (Matthew 13:36-43)

> In that place there will be weeping and gnashing of teeth, when you see Abraham and Isaac and Jacob and all the prophets in the kingdom of God but you yourselves cast out. And people will come from east and west, and from north and south, and recline at table in the kingdom of God. (Luke 13:28-29)

28 Philippians 2:11

29 I am deeply indebted to the scholarly work of George Eldon Ladd on the Kingdom of God in the New Testament. See George Eldon Ladd, *A Theology of the New Testament* (Grand Rapids, MI: William B. Eerdmans Publishing Co., revised 1993), chapters 4-9.

[30] There are also many passages that speak of the Kingdom as a present reality. See, for example:

> Blessed are the poor in spirit, for theirs is the kingdom of heaven. (Matthew 5:3)

> Blessed are those who are persecuted for righteousness' sake, for theirs is the kingdom of heaven (Matthew 5:10)

> But seek first the kingdom of God and his righteousness, and all these things will be added to you. (Matthew 6:33)

> Truly, I say to you, among those born of women there has arisen no one greater than John the Baptist. Yet the one who is least in the kingdom of heaven is greater than he. From the days of John the Baptist until now the kingdom of heaven has suffered violence, and the violent take it by force. For all the Prophets and the Law prophesied until John. (Matthew 11:11-13)

> But if it is by the Spirit of God that I cast out demons, then the kingdom of God has come upon you. (Matthew 12:28)

> Which of the two did the will of his father?" They said, "The first." Jesus said to them, "Truly, I say to you, the tax collectors and the prostitutes go into the kingdom of God before you. (Matthew 21:31)

> But woe to you, scribes and Pharisees, hypocrites! For you shut the kingdom of heaven in people's faces. For you neither enter yourselves nor allow those who would enter to go in. (Matthew 23:13)

> The time is fulfilled, and the kingdom of God is at hand; repent and believe in the gospel. (Mark 1:15)

> But when Jesus saw it, he was indignant and said to them, "Let the children come to me; do not hinder them, for to such belongs the kingdom of God. Truly, I say to you, whoever does not receive the kingdom of God like a child shall not enter it." (Mark 10:14-15)

> Being asked by the Pharisees when the kingdom of God would come, he answered them, "The kingdom of God is not coming in ways that can be observed." (Luke 17:20)

CHAPTER 2: UNDERSTANDING THE KINGDOM

[1] "Jesus answered him [Pilate], "You would have no authority over me at all unless it had been given you from above. Therefore he who delivered me over to you has the greater sin." (John 19:11)

[2] See:

> Let every person be subject to the governing authorities. For there is no authority except from God, and those that exist have been instituted by God. Therefore whoever resists the authorities resists what God has appointed, and those who resist will incur judgment. For rulers are not a terror to good conduct, but to bad. Would you have no fear of the one who is in ? Then do what is good, and you will receive his approval, for he is God's servant for your good. But if you do wrong, be afraid, for he does not bear the sword in vain. For he is the servant of God, an avenger who carries out God's wrath on the wrongdoer. Therefore one must be in subjection, not only to avoid God's wrath but also for the sake of conscience. For because of this you also pay taxes, for the authorities are ministers of God, attending to this very thing. Pay to all what is owed to them: taxes to whom taxes are owed, revenue to whom revenue is owed, respect to whom respect is owed, honor to whom honor is owed. (Romans 13:1-7)

Government is an agent of common grace; the Kingdom of God is redemptive grace in action. In our fallen world, government often seems to be as much a part of the problem as it is part of the solution. That does not negate its ordination and calling from God to restrain and mitigate sin in our social environments, and to preserve peace, stability, and order in our fallen world. It means that it is in need of reform. If they are called by God to do so, and they fulfill their calling for the glory of God and the good of others, followers of Christ can play that reforming role. It is not only true that common grace can serve the purposes of redemptive grace (by protecting the innocent, preserving peace, and promoting the welfare of citizens and sojourners), redemptive grace at work in the redeemed can transform the institutions of common grace.

It is also true that governments can so subvert and oppose their charter from God that we must oppose them to be true to God's Kingdom:

> And when they had brought them, they set them before the council. And the high priest questioned them, saying, "We strictly charged you not to teach in this name, yet here you have filled Jerusalem with your teaching, and you intend to bring this man's blood upon us." But Peter and the apostles answered, "We must obey God rather than men." (Acts 5:27-29)

[3] Roman roads and the *Pax Romana* facilitated Christian missionary work in the first century. Many similar instances could be cited throughout history and in the modern world.

[4] The role of government in structural evil and the political implications of the Gospel should be addressed by agents of the Kingdom in word and deed. Reforming

government is a worthy enterprise. However, and more fundamentally, I believe that French political philosopher Alexis de Tocqueville was right when he said, "In democracy we get the government we deserve." Government leaders not only represent the electorate, they reflect it. They come from us. They are products of the culture that all of us have helped shape with our beliefs, values, and the manner in which we live. Real and lasting change in democratic governments will occur only as citizens are transformed and their culture is renovated by the values of the Kingdom. Heal the tree and its fruit will be healthy (Matthew 12:33).

5   See the following:

> Pilate then called together the chief priests and the *rulers* and the people. (Luke 23:13)

> And the people stood by, watching, but the *rulers* scoffed at him, saying, "He saved others; let him save himself, if he is the Christ of God, his Chosen One!" (Luke 23:35)

> Our chief priests and *rulers* delivered him up to be condemned to death and crucified him. (Luke 24:40)

> And now, brothers, I know that you acted in ignorance, as did also your *rulers*. (Acts 3:17)

> The kings of the earth set themselves, and the *rulers* were gathered together, against the Lord and against his Anointed. (Acts 4:26)

> For those who live in Jerusalem and their *rulers*, because they did not recognize him nor understand the utterances of the prophets, which are read every Sabbath, fulfilled them by condemning him. (Acts 13:27)

> None of the *rulers* of this age understood this, for if they had, they would not have crucified the Lord of glory. (1 Corinthians 2:8)

6   "For whoever would save his life will lose it, but whoever loses his life for my sake and the gospel's will save it." (Mark 8:35)

7   "But it shall not be so among you. But whoever would be great among you must be your servant, and whoever would be first among you must be slave of all." (Mark 10:43-44)

8   See:

> Where is the one who is wise? Where is the scribe? Where is the debater of this age? Has
> not God made foolish the wisdom of the world? For since, in the wisdom of God, the
> world did not know God through wisdom, it pleased God through the folly of what we
> preach to save those who believe. For Jews demand signs and Greeks seek wisdom, but
> we preach Christ crucified, a stumbling block to Jews and folly to Gentiles, but to those
> who are called, both Jews and Greeks, Christ the power of God and the wisdom of
> God. For the foolishness of God is wiser than men, and the weakness of God is
> stronger than men. (I Corinthians 1:20-25)

9   "But God chose what is foolish in the world to shame the wise; God chose what is weak
in the world to shame the strong; God chose what is low and despised in the world, even
things that are not, to bring to nothing things that are, so that no human being might
boast in the presence of God." (1 Corinthians 1:27-29)

10   "Then the seventh angel blew his trumpet, and there were loud voices in heaven, saying,
'The kingdom of the world has become the kingdom of our Lord and of his Christ, and
he shall reign forever and ever.'" (Revelation 11:15)

11   Which is why we should hope to see many followers of Christ in civic leadership! Their
role in government is to be an agent of common grace; their *presence* in government as
followers of Christ should be an agency for redemptive grace; agency for the Kingdom.

12   He goes on to say:

> The first political task of the Church is to be the Church. That is, Christians must
> proclaim and demonstrate the Gospel to all people, embracing them in a sustaining
> community of faith and discipline under the Lordship of Christ. In obedience to this
> biblical mandate, Christians have a special care for all who are in need, especially the
> poor, the oppressed, the despised and the marginal. The Church is called to be a
> community of diversity, including people of every race, nation, class, and political
> viewpoint. As a universal community, the Church witnesses to the limits of the national
> and ideological loyalties that divide mankind. Communal allegiance to Christ and his
> Kingdom is the indispensable check upon pretensions of the modern state. Because
> Christ is Lord, Caesar is not Lord. By humbling all secular claims to sovereignty, the
> Church makes its most important political contribution by being, fully and
> unapologetically, the Church.

Richard John Neuhaus, "Christianity and Democracy." Online version found at:
http://www.leaderu.com/ftissues/ft9610/articles/documentation.html

13   It is commonplace to hear exaggerations of the role of Deism in the American colonies.
Harvard historian, Perry Miller, contests this: "European Deism was an exotic plant in
America, which never struck roots in the soil. 'Rationalism' was never so widespread as
liberal historians, or those fascinated by Jefferson, have imagined." Perry Miller,

Nature's Nation (Cambridge, MA: Belknap Press of Harvard University Press, first edition, 1967), p. 110.

[14] See the October 9, 2012 study by The Pew Research Center, "'Nones' on the Rise: One-in-Five Adults Have No Religious Affiliation" at http://www.pewforum.org/2012/10/09/nones-on-the-rise. Some refer to these "Nones" as a new generation of Deists.

Philip Ryken, President of Wheaton College, says that Deism "may be one of the most common worldviews in America today." Philip Graham Ryken, *Christian Worldview: A Student's Guide* (Wheaton, IL: Crossway, 2013), p. 35.

[15] The book *Soul Searching: The Religious and Spiritual Lives of American Teenagers*, by sociologists Christian Smith and Melinda Lundquist Denton, introduced the term "Moral Therapeutic Deism" to describe the faith of many teenagers in the United States. The authors say:

> . . . it appears to us, another popular religious faith, Moralistic Therapeutic Deism, is colonizing many historical religious traditions and, almost without anyone noticing, converting believers in the old faiths to its alternative religious vision of divinely underwritten personal happiness and interpersonal niceness. . . . we have come with some confidence to believe that a significant part of Christianity in the United States is actually only tenuously Christian in any sense that is seriously connected to the actual historical Christian tradition, but has rather substantially morphed into Christianity's misbegotten stepcousin, Christian Moralistic Therapeutic Deism. . . . The language, and therefore experience, of Trinity, holiness, sin, grace, justification, sanctification, church, Eucharist, and heaven and hell, appear, among most Christian teenagers in the United States at the very least, to be supplanted by the language of happiness, niceness, and an earned heavenly reward. It is not so much that U.S. Christianity is being secularized. Rather, more subtly, Christianity is either degenerating into a pathetic version of itself or, more significantly, Christianity is actively being colonized and displaced by a quite different religious faith.

Christian Smith with Melinda Lundquist Denton, *Soul Searching: The Religious and Spiritual Lives of American Teenagers* (Oxford: Oxford University Press, 2005), p. 171.

[16] Because we are creatures who are embedded in space and time, our language necessarily reflects this. When we speak of God or other beings or states of affairs that are not part of our physical world, we are limited to the language we have. But we can be aware of those limitations, and let that awareness shape our understanding of things.

The Bible uses spatial language about God and the spiritual realm. For instance, we find the terms "high" and "above" when the Bible addresses heavenly realities.

> Be exalted, O God, above the heavens! Let your glory be over all the earth! (Psalm 57:11)

Glory to God in the highest, and on earth peace among those with whom he is pleased! (Luke 2:14)

Set your mind on the things above, not on the things that are on earth. (Colossians 3:2)

[That you may know] the immeasurable greatness of his power toward us who believe, according to the working of his great might that he worked in Christ when he raised him from the dead and seated him at his right hand in the heavenly places, far above all rule and authority and power and dominion, and above every name that is named, not only in this age but also in the one to come. (Ephesians 20-21)

This language conveys the very important truths of the transcendence and majesty of God. He is not trapped by our world, or limited by it in any way. Similarly, heaven is "above" our realm of suffering and pain, and neither participates in nor is impacted by the sin of the world.

But the Bible also uses visual metaphors – visible and invisible, seen and unseen – to describe the same things. This suggests that spiritual realities are not somewhere else (literally above us, looking down on us), they are all around us, but invisible to us.

We look not to the things that are seen but to the things that are unseen. For the things that are seen are transient, but the things that are unseen are eternal. (2 Corinthians 4:18)

For by him all things were created, in heaven and on earth, visible and invisible, whether thrones or dominions or rulers or authorities—all things were created through him and for him. (Colossians 1:16)

For we do not wrestle against flesh and blood, but against the rulers, against the authorities, against the cosmic powers over this present darkness, against the spiritual forces of evil in the heavenly places. (Ephesians 6:12)

By faith [Moses] left Egypt, not being afraid of the anger of the king, for he endured as seeing him who is invisible. (Hebrews 11:27)

[17] Robert Kolb and Timothy J. Wenger eds. *The Book of Concord: The Confessions of the Evangelical Lutheran Church*, trans. Charles Arand, et al (Minneapolis: Fortress Press, 2000), p. 22.

[18] If there is a story in the Scriptures that teaches us this truth about the world, it is a tale about Elisha. The prophet's home was surrounded by Syrian soldiers, committed to his demise. Panicked, his servant came to him with this dire news. Elisha responded that there was no need for fear because "Those who are with us are more than those who are with them." His servant saw nothing but physical terrain and enemy troops bent on their destruction. Elisha prayed that the LORD would open his servant's eyes. This is

where we pick up the story: "So the LORD opened the eyes of the young man, and he saw, and behold, the mountain was full of horses and chariots of fire all around Elisha." This heavenly army was not dispatched from somewhere else. They were already there, unseen until God made them manifest.

> When the servant of the man of God rose early in the morning and went out, behold, an army with horses and chariots was all around the city. And the servant said, 'Alas, my master! What shall we do?' He said, 'Do not be afraid, for those who are with us are more than those who are with them.' Then Elisha prayed and said, 'O LORD, please open his eyes that he may see.' So the LORD opened the eyes of the young man, and he saw, and behold, the mountain was full of horses and chariots of fire all around Elisha. (2 Kings 6: 15-17)

[19] This is the way ancient believers saw the world. C.S. Lewis wrote:

> The reason why the modern literalist is puzzled is that he is trying to get out of the old writers something which is not there. Starting from a clear modern distinction between material and immaterial he tries to find out on which side of that distinction the ancient Hebrew conception fell. He forgets that the distinction itself has been made clear only by later thought.

C.S. Lewis, *Miracles: A Preliminary Study* (New York, NY: HarperOne, 1996), p. 122. See also:

> [On the writing of *Perelandra* and contemplating "a creature like an eldil."] The distinction between natural and supernatural, in fact, broke down; and when it had done so, one realised how great a comfort it had been – how it had eased the burden of intolerable strangeness which this universe imposes on us by dividing it into two halves and encouraging the mind never to think of both in the same context. What price we may have paid for this comfort in the way of false security and accepted confusion of thought is another matter.

C.S. Lewis, *Perelandra*, (New York, NY: Scribner, 1996), p. 11.

[20] Matthew 3:2

[21] Luke 10:9

[22] Luke 17:21-22

[23] Matthew 12:28

[24] To learn more about the New Testament concept of the Kingdom of God see George Eldon Ladd, *A Theology of the New Testament* (Grand Rapids, MI: William B. Eerdmans Publishing Co., revised 1993) chapters 4-9.

²⁵ "For we do not wrestle against flesh and blood, but against the rulers, against the authorities, against the cosmic powers over this present darkness, against the spiritual forces of evil in the heavenly places. " (Ephesians 6:12)

²⁶ "Therefore, since we are surrounded by so great a cloud of witnesses, let us also lay aside every weight, and sin which clings so closely, and let us run with endurance the race that is set before us." (Hebrews 12:1)

²⁷ I am reminded of the story of J.B. Phillips, the New Testament scholar and translator, who had an experience in which C.S. Lewis, shortly after his death, reportedly appeared to him twice in his home "ruddier in complexion than ever, grinning all over his face and, as the old-fashioned saying has it, positively glowing with health." Here is Phillips' account:

> A few days after his death, while I was watching television, he "appeared" sitting in a chair within a few feet of me, and spoke a few works which were particularly relevant to the difficult circumstances through which I was passing. He was ruddier in complexion than ever, grinning all over his face, and, as the old-fashioned saying has it, positively glowing with health. The interesting thing to me was that I had not been thinking about him at all. I was neither alarmed nor surprised nor . . . did I look up to see the hole in the ceiling that he might have made on arrival! He was just *there* -- "large as life and twice as natural." A week later, this time when I was in bed, reading before going to sleep, he appeared again, even more rosily radiant than before, and repeated to me the same message, which was very important to me at the time. I was a little puzzled by this, and I mentioned it to a certain saintly bishop who was then living in retirement here in Dorset. His reply was, "My dear J---, this sort of thing is happening all the time."

J.B. Phillips, *Ring of Truth: A Translator's Testimony*, New York: Macmillan Co., 1967), pp. 118-119.

²⁸ John 3:3

²⁹ ". . . having the eyes of your hearts enlightened, that you may know what is the hope to which he has called you, what are the riches of his glorious inheritance in the saints." (Ephesians 1:18)

³⁰ C.S. Lewis wrote, "The Supernatural is not remote and abstruse: it is a matter of daily and hourly experience: as intimate as breathing." C.S. Lewis, *Miracles*, p. 65.

³¹ The human soul cannot be reduced to the physical properties of our brains and our bodies. We were created with a transcendent dimension, a supernatural dimension, that links us not only to the material world but to supernatural reality. When we become a habitation for God's Spirit in his work of redemption, we live in an existential interface with the supernatural world.

[32] See, for example:

> For I tell you, unless your righteousness exceeds that of the scribes and Pharisees, you will never enter the kingdom of heaven. (Matthew 5:20)

> Not everyone who says to me, 'Lord, Lord,' will enter the kingdom of heaven, but the one who does the will of my Father who is in heaven. (Matthew 7:21)

> Truly, I say to you, unless you turn and become like children, you will never enter the kingdom of heaven. (Matthew 18:3)

> Truly, I say to you, only with difficulty will a rich person enter the kingdom of heaven. (Matthew 19:23)

> But woe to you, scribes and Pharisees, hypocrites! For you shut the kingdom of heaven in people's faces. For you neither enter yourselves nor allow those who would enter to go in. (Matthew 23:13)

[33] Mark 1:14-15

[34] The Greek word for repentance, *metanoia*, literally means a "change of mind." Gerhard Kittel, ed., *Theological Dictionary of the New Testament*, trans. Geoffrey W. Bromiley (Grand Rapids, MI: Wm. B. Eerdmans Publishing Co., 1964), Vol. IV, p. 978. It is a radical change of mind and change of heart that leads to a change in direction and a changed life.

[35] You can read the parable in full in Luke 15:11-32.

[36] See:

> For not only has the word of the Lord sounded forth from you in Macedonia and Achaia, but your faith in God has gone forth everywhere, so that we need not say anything. For they themselves report concerning us the kind of reception we had among you, and how you turned to God from idols to serve *the living and true God.*" (1 Thessalonians 1:8-9)

[37] C.S. Lewis, *Reflections on the Psalms* (New York: Harcourt Brace Jovanovich, 1958) p. 32.

It is true that the Scriptures sometimes speak of God's hatred of sinners (e.g., Psalm 5:4-6), but, in light of other clear statements about God's love for sinners, we should interpret those passages to mean that he hates the wicked *with respect to* their wickedness, the evil *with respect to* their evil, and sinners *with respect to* their sin.

C.S. Lewis wrote:

I remember Christian teachers telling me long ago that I must hate a bad man's actions, but not hate the bad man: or, as they would say, hate the sin but not the sinner. For a long time I used to think this a silly, straw-splitting distinction: how could you hate what a man did and not hate the man? But years later it occurred to me that there was one man to whom I had been doing this all my life – namely myself. However much I might dislike my own cowardice or conceit or greed, I went on loving myself. There had never been the slightest difficulty about it. In fact the very reason why I hated the things was that I loved the man. Just because I loved myself, I was sorry to find that I was the sort of man who did those things. Consequently, Christianity does not want us to reduce by one atom the hatred we feel for cruelty and treachery. We ought to hate them. Not one word of what we have said about them needs to be unsaid. But it does want us to hate them in the same way in which we hate things in ourselves: being sorry that the man should have done such things, and hoping, if it is anyway possible, that somehow, sometime, somewhere he can be cured and made human again.

C.S. Lewis, *Mere Christianity* (New York: Harper Collins, 2001), p. 117.

[38] Luther's Ninety-five Theses began with this assertion: "When our Lord and Master Jesus Christ said 'Repent,' he intended that the entire life of believers should be repentance." See *Luther's Works*, ed., Harold J. Grim, (Philadelphia: Muhlenberg Press, 1957), Vol. 31, p. 25.

[39] The apostle Paul contrasts those whose sin keeps them from the Kingdom of God with those in whom the fruit of the Spirit grows:

> Now the works of the flesh are evident: sexual immorality, impurity, sensuality, idolatry, sorcery, enmity, strife, jealousy, fits of anger, rivalries, dissensions, divisions, envy, drunkenness, orgies, and things like these. I warn you, as I warned you before, *that those who do such things will not inherit the kingdom of God. But the fruit of the Spirit is love, joy, peace, patience, kindness, goodness, faithfulness, gentleness, self-control*; against such things there is no law. (Galatians 5:19-23)

[40] 1 Corinthians 4:20

[41] Acts 10:38

[42] See also:

> My speech and my message were not in plausible words of wisdom, but in demonstration of the Spirit and of power. (1 Corinthians 2:4)

> For the weapons of our warfare are not of the flesh but have divine power to destroy strongholds. (2 Corinthians 10:4)

> But he said to me, "My grace is sufficient for you, for my power is made perfect in weakness." Therefore I will boast all the more gladly of my weaknesses, so that the power of Christ may rest upon me. (2 Corinthians 12:9)

[43] Rick Howe, *Path of Life: Finding the Joy You've Always Longed For* (Boulder, CO: University Ministries Press, Revised Edition, 2017), p. 48.

[44] See Romans 14:17.

[45] Roland Bainton, *Here I Stand*, p. 377. Luther applied this truth to his own battles with despondency, but it has a much broader application.

[46] I am reminded of the legendary sword of Charlemagne, "Joyeus," or "joyful one."

CHAPTER 3: THE KINGDOM AT WORK

[1] Isaiah prophesied of the Messiah:

> For to us a child is born,
>   to us a son is given;
>   and *the government shall be upon his shoulder*,
> and his name shall be called
>   Wonderful Counselor, Mighty God,
>   Everlasting Father, Prince of Peace.
> Of the increase of his government and of peace
>   there will be no end,
> on the throne of David and over his kingdom,
>   to establish it and to uphold it with justice and with righteousness
>   from this time forth and forevermore.
> The zeal of the LORD of hosts will do this. (Isaiah 9:6-7)

[2] With traditional ending.

[3] Henri Nouwen wrote, "When prayer is no longer its primary concern, and when its many activities are no longer seen and experienced as part of prayer itself, the community quickly degenerates into a club with a common cause but no common vocation." Henri J.M. Nouwen, *Reaching Out: The Three Movements of the Spiritual Life* (New York: Doubleday, 1975), p. 156.

[4] Romans 14:17

[5] This is taught vividly in the story of Joshua before the gates of Jericho:

> When Joshua was by Jericho, he lifted up his eyes and looked, and behold, a man was standing before him with his drawn sword in his hand. And Joshua went to him and said to him, "Are you for us, or for our adversaries?" And he said, "No; but I am the commander of the army of the LORD. Now I have come." And Joshua fell on his face to the earth and worshiped and said to him, "What does my lord say to his servant?" And the commander of the LORD's army said to Joshua, "Take off your sandals from

your feet, for the place where you are standing is holy." And Joshua did so. (Joshua 5:13-15).

6   Charles Hodge, *Commentary on the Epistle to the Romans* (Grand Rapids, MI: William B. Eerdmans Publishing Co., Rev. ed., 1886, reprint. 1980), p. 424.

7   Romans 14:18, literal translation.

8   See the preceding verses:

> Then let us no more pass judgment on one another, but rather decide never to put a stumbling block or hindrance in the way of a brother. I know and am persuaded in the Lord Jesus that nothing is unclean in itself; but it is unclean for any one who thinks it unclean. If your brother is being injured by what you eat, you are no longer walking in love. Do not let what you eat cause the ruin of one for whom Christ died. So do not let your good be spoken of as evil. For the kingdom of God is not food and drink . . . . (Romans 14:13-17)

9   C.E.B. Cranfield, *A Critical and Exegetical Commentary on The Epistle to the Romans* (Edinburgh: T&T Clark Limited, 1979, reprint. 1981), Vol. 2, p. 718.

10   C.K. Barrett, *A Commentary on the Epistle to the Romans* (New York: Harper & Row Publishers, 1957), p. 265.

If we let Paul speak for himself, and speak his mind fully, he sees righteousness both as a judicial standing before God, and as action that seeks the well-being of others before God. The first is his doctrine of justification ("righteousness by faith") and is especially in view in chapters 3-5 of his letter to the Romans. The second is a "righteousness leading to sanctification" (e.g., Romans 6:13, 16, 18, 19), and includes the many practical exhortations that seek the good of others in Romans 12-14.

11   See the following:

> For I have chosen him, that he may command his children and his household after him to keep the way of the LORD by *doing righteousness* and justice, so that the Lord may bring to Abraham what he has promised him." (Genesis 18:19)
> Blessed are they who observe justice, who *do righteousness* at all times! (Psalm 106:3)

> To *do righteousness* and justice is more acceptable to the LORD than sacrifice. (Proverbs 21:3)

> Thus says the LORD: "Keep justice, and *do righteousness*, for soon my salvation will come, and my righteousness be revealed. (Isaiah 56:1)

> Thus says the LORD: *Do justice and righteousness*, and deliver from the hand of the oppressor him who has been robbed. (Jeremiah 22:3)

[12] Contextually, Paul is concerned with those who "put a stumbling block or hindrance in the way of a brother" (14:13, RSV). If righteousness is action taken to help others flourish before God, then acting in ways that cause others to fall is a direct contradiction to this. The positive commitment to righteousness in this sense is found, for instance, in 14:19 – "Let us then pursue what makes for peace and for mutual up building," (RSV) and in 15:2, "Let each of us please his neighbor for his good, to edify him." (RSV)

[13] Psalm 97:2

[14] From the beginning of the human project, God exercises dominion in developing the world through human agents. This is true of the "cultural mandate" given in creation, and it is true in our era of the Kingdom.

[15] NIV. You can see from these passages that the biblical concepts of righteousness and justice overlap. Biblical justice is not the same as the classical Greek understanding of this moral quality. In its Aristotelian sense, justice is calculating and disinterested. It is giving a person his due. From a biblical perspective the just person is not merely one who acts justly because it is required of him; he desires justice, loves justice, and delights in justice. It is not disinterested or detached, but passionately involved. It is not giving a person his due on the basis of merit, but acting in ways that will promote human flourishing as an expression of love.

Donald Bloesch writes:

> Both humanitarian works of mercy and works of social reform are at best approximations of kingdom righteousness. If the church identified itself with the cause of social justice, this might indeed make people more receptive to the kingdom message. Social justice is a partial fulfillment of the law of God; the eschatological kingdom is the perfect fulfillment of the teachings of the law. Social justice is related to the law of God; the righteousness of the kingdom is related to the gospel. Social justice is conducive to human happiness; Christian obedience brings blessedness – contagious, radiant joy.

Donald G. Bloesch, *Freedom for Obedience: Evangelical Ethics in Contemporary Times* (San Francisco: Harper and Row, 1987), p. 84.

[16] Joy is both a centrifugal and a centripetal spiritual force: It reaches out and draws others in. Joy is hospitable: always seeking company and inviting and bringing others home to share its boon. Our own joy is enhanced, enriched, and enlarged as we give ourselves to its largess. James Gilman puts this into the context of our concern for the poor, "The community's joy lies in the privilege of sharing with the poor the same gracious kindness it receives from God, so that in the end both donor and recipient rejoice together." James E. Gilman, *Fidelity of the Heart, An Ethic of Christian Virtue* (Oxford: Oxford University Press, 2001), p. 61.

17 See his teaching on this matter recorded in Matthew 25:31-40:

> When the Son of Man comes in his glory, and all the angels with him, then he will sit on his glorious throne. Before him will be gathered all the nations, and he will separate people one from another as a shepherd separates the sheep from the goats. And he will place the sheep on his right, but the goats on the left. Then the King will say to those on his right, "Come, you who are blessed by my Father, inherit the kingdom prepared for you from the foundation of the world. For I was hungry and you gave me food, I was thirsty and you gave me drink, I was a stranger and you welcomed me, I was naked and you clothed me, I was sick and you visited me, I was in prison and you came to me." Then the righteous will answer him, saying, "Lord, when did we see you hungry and feed you, or thirsty and give you drink? And when did we see you a stranger and welcome you, or naked and clothe you? And when did we see you sick or in prison and visit you?" And the King will answer them, "Truly, I say to you, as you did it to one of the least of these my brothers, you did it to me."

18 "Let us then pursue what makes for peace and for mutual upbuilding." (Romans 14:19, RSV)

19 Romans 12:18

20 *Shalom* is a prominent theme in Isaiah:

> For to us a child is born,
>   to us a son is given;
> and the government shall be upon his shoulder,
>   and his name shall be called
> Wonderful Counselor, Mighty God,
>   Everlasting Father, Prince of *Peace*.
> Of the increase of his government and of *peace*
>   there will be no end,
> on the throne of David and over his kingdom,
>   to establish it and to uphold it
> with justice and with righteousness
>   from this time forth and forevermore.
> The zeal of the LORD of hosts will do this. (9:6-7)

> You keep him in perfect *peace*
>   whose mind is stayed on you,
> because he trusts in you. (26:1)

> O LORD, you will ordain *peace* for us,
>   for you have indeed done for us all our works. (26:12)

> And the effect of righteousness will be *peace*,
>   and the result of righteousness, quietness and trust forever.
> My people will abide in a *peaceful* habitation,

in secure dwellings, and in quiet resting places. (32:17-18)

Oh that you had paid attention to my commandments!
Then your *peace* would have been like a river,
  and your righteousness like the waves of the sea; (48:18)

How beautiful upon the mountains
  are the feet of him who brings good news,
who publishes *peace*, who brings good news of happiness,
  who publishes salvation,
  who says to Zion, "Your God reigns." (52:7)

For the mountains may depart
  and the hills be removed,
but my steadfast love shall not depart from you,
  and my covenant of *peace* shall not be removed,"
  says the LORD, who has compassion on you. (54:10)

"For you shall go out in joy
  and be led forth in *peace*;
the mountains and the hills before you
  shall break forth into singing,
  and all the trees of the field shall clap their hands. (55:12)

I have seen his ways, but I will heal him;
  I will lead him and restore comfort to him and his mourners,
  creating the fruit of the lips.
Peace, peace, to the far and to the near," says the LORD,
  "and I will heal him. (57:18-19)

[21] Cornelius Plantinga, Jr., *Not the Way It's Supposed to Be: A Breviary of Sin*, (Grand Rapids, MI: William B. Eerdmans Publishing Company, 1995), p.10.

[22] "Healthy joy cannot be full while sisters and brothers are in misery. Joy in a surrounding context of misery is insulted and undone." Daniel C. Maguire, *The Moral Core of Judaism and Christianity: Reclaiming the Revolution* (Minneapolis: Fortress Press, 1993), p. 279.

[23] See Isaiah 32:17-18.

  And *the effect of righteousness will be peace*,
    and the result of righteousness, quietness and trust forever.
  My people will abide in a peaceful habitation,
    in secure dwellings, and in quiet resting places.

[24] Gilman, *Fidelity of Heart:* p. 54.

[25] In this context, joy as the consummation of *shalom*:

> It is "the fulfillment of our capacity for rejoicing." Maguire, *Moral Core*, p. 236.
> It is to "enjoy living before God, to enjoy living in nature, to enjoy living with one's fellows, to enjoy life with oneself." Nicholas Wolterstorff, *Art in Action: Toward a Christian Aesthetic* (Grand Rapids: Eerdmans, 1980), p. 79.
>
> It is "a just peace with joy in God's creation." Bloesch, *Freedom for Obedience*, p. 90.

[26] For a discussion of the kingdom of God as both indicative and imperative for the Christian life, see George Eldon Ladd, *A Theology of the New Testament* (Grand Rapids, MI: William B. Eerdmans Publishing Co., 1974), pp. 524-525.

[27] Emil Brunner wrote, "A Christian is a person who not only hopes for the Kingdom of God, but one who, because he hopes for it, also does something in this world already, which he who has not this hope does not do." Emil Brunner, *The Divine Imperative*, trans. Olive Wyon, (The Westminster Press: Philadelphia, 1947), p. 128.

[28] Cornelius Plantinga writes:

> But we have also been called, and graced, to delight in our lives, to feel their irony and angularity, to make something sturdy and even lovely of them. For such undertakings, we have to find emotional and spiritual funding from the very God who assigns them, turning our faces toward God's light so that we may be drawn to it, warmed by it, bathed in it, revitalized by it. Then we have to find our role within God's big project, the one that stretches across the border from this life into the next. To be a responsible person is to find one's role in the building of shalom, the re-webbing of God, humanity, and all creation in justice, harmony, fulfillment, and delight. To be a responsible person is to find one's own role and then, funded by the grace of God, to fill this role and to delight in it.

Plantinga, *Not the Way It's Supposed to Be*, p. 197.

[29] There was much more to the Fundamentalist-Modernist controversy than this. For an overview, see George M. Marsden, *Fundamentalism and American Culture*. 2nd ed. (New York: Oxford University Press, 2006)

[30] H. Richard Niebuhr wrote, "Maurice had a principle, gained from J.S. Mill, that commends itself to us. He affirmed that men were generally right in what they affirmed, and wrong in what they denied." H. Richard Niebuhr, *Christ and Culture* (New York, New York: Harper and Row, 1951), p. 238.

[31] The way for this was paved by Carl F.H. Henry, one of the pioneers of evangelicalism, and his seminal work, *The Uneasy Conscience of Modern Fundamentalism* (Grand Rapids, Wm. B. Eerdmans Publishing Company 1947).

32   For a review of the nature and significance of good works, see the section "Work as a Good Work" in Rick Howe, *River of Delights: Quenching Your Thirst For Joy, Volume 2* (Boulder, CO: University Ministries Press, 2017), Chapter 3.

33   James Gilman puts this into the context of our concern for the poor, "The community's joy lies in the privilege of sharing with the poor the same gracious kindness it receives from God, so that in the end both donor and recipient rejoice together." Gilman, *Fidelity of Heart*, p. 61.

34   "Indeed, joy is a primary emotional force without which love's project of sorrowing with the poor, is unlikely to be accomplished." Ibid., p. 60.

35   David Gill writes, "Our hunger for righteousness and our peacemaking have too often been accompanied by the long, sad face, the angry denunciation, and a holier-than-thou, sanctimonious spirituality. The Bible doesn't know this grumpy righteousness: 'Rejoice in the LORD, O you righteous.'" David W. Gill, *Becoming Good: Building Moral Character* (Downers Grove, Illinois: InterVarsity Press, 2000), p. 200.

36   The Greek word translated "cheerfully" is *hilaros*, from which we get the word *hilarious*.

37   It is the Greek word *hilaros* again.

38   Malcolm Muggeridge, *Something Beautiful for God; Mother Teresa of Calcutta* (New York, Harper and Row, Publishers, 1971, p. 52.

39   Ibid., p. 49. In his recorded interview with her, Muggeridge comments: "Spending a few days with you, I have been immensely struck by the joyfulness of these Sisters who do what an outsider might think to be an almost impossibly difficult and painful task." Her response:

> That's the spirit of our society, that total surrender, loving trust and cheerfulness. We must be able to radiate the joy of Christ, express it in our actions. If our actions are just useful actions that give no joy to the people, our poor people would never be able to rise up to the call which we want them to hear, the call to come closer to God. We want to make them feel that they are loved. If we went to them with a sad face, we would only make them much more depressed.

Ibid., p. 98.

Another wrote of Mother Teresa:

> More and more every day I realized the importance of Mother Teresa's insistence that the Missionaries of Charity renounce gloominess along with everything else of the world. She requires that the Sisters be persons of cheerful disposition in their work with

people who lead deprived lives. "A joyful Sister," she says, "is like the sunshine of God's love."

"Joy," affirms the guideline of the Society, "is a net of love by which we catch souls. A Sister filled with joy preaches without preaching. Joy is a need and a power for us even physically, for it makes us always ready to go about doing good. The joy of the Lord is our strength."
When one of the Sisters, wearing a mournful expression on her face, was getting ready to visit the poor, Mother Teresa said, "Don't go. Go back to bed. We cannot meet the poor with sad faces."

Eileen Egan and Kathleen Egan, OSB, *Suffering Into Joy: What Mother Teresa Teaches About True Joy* (Ann Arbor, MI: Servant Publications, 1994), pp. 45-46.

[40] "Let your light so shine before men, that they may see your good works and give glory to your Father who is in heaven." (Matthew 5:16)

CHAPTER 4: KINGDOM AGENTS

[1] See the following:

> For you did not receive the spirit of slavery to fall back into fear, but you have received the Spirit of adoption as sons, by whom we cry, "Abba! Father!" (Romans 8:15)

> "The Spirit himself bears witness with our spirit that we are children of God, and if children, then heirs—heirs of God and fellow heirs with Christ. . . . (Romans 8:16-17)
> And not only the creation, but we ourselves, who have the firstfruits of the Spirit, groan inwardly as we wait eagerly for adoption as sons, the redemption of our bodies. (Romans 8:23)

> . . . to redeem those who were under the law, so that we might receive adoption as sons. (Galatians 4:5)

> He predestined us for adoption as sons through Jesus Christ, according to the purpose of his will. (Ephesians 1:5)

[2] "For those whom he foreknew he also predestined to be conformed to the image of his Son, in order that he might be the firstborn among many brothers." (Romans 8:29)

[3] See:

> In him we have obtained an inheritance, having been predestined according to the purpose of him who works all things according to the counsel of his will, so that we who were the first to hope in Christ might be to the praise of his glory. In him you also, when you heard the word of truth, the gospel of your salvation, and believed in him,

were sealed with the promised Holy Spirit, who is the guarantee of our inheritance until we acquire possession of it, to the praise of his glory. (Matthew 12:27-29)

[4]   See:

This is evidence of the righteous judgment of God, that you may be considered worthy of the kingdom of God, for which you are also suffering. (2 Thessalonians 1:5)

So as to walk in a manner worthy of the Lord, fully pleasing to him, bearing fruit in every good work and increasing in the knowledge of God. (Colossians 1:10)

[5]   N.T. Wright, *Simply Christian: Why Christianity Makes Sense* (U.S.A.: HarperSanFrancisco, 2006), p. 92.

[6]   Whether one agrees with his claim about a Christian consensus in the past, I think his analysis of the contemporary Church, and his warnings about the future, are spot-on.

[7]   Francis A. Schaeffer, *How Should We Then Live? The Rise and Decline of Western Thought and Culture* (Old Tappan, New Jersey: Fleming H. Revell Company, 1976), p. 205ff.

Christopher Lasch saw and said something similar:

After the political turmoil of the sixties, Americans have retreated to purely personal preoccupations. Having no hope of improving their lives in any of the ways that matter, people have convinced themselves that what matters is psychic self-improvement: getting in touch with their feelings, eating health food, taking lessons in ballet or belly-dancing, immersing themselves in the wisdom of the East, jogging, learning how to "relate," overcoming the "fear of pleasure."

The contemporary climate is therapeutic, not religious. People today hunger not for personal satisfaction, let alone for the restoration of an earlier age, but for the feeling, the momentary illusion, of personal well-being, health and psychic security.

Christopher Lasch, *The Culture of Narcissism* (New York: Norton, 1978), pp. 4, 7.

[8]   It was said of David as a young man, 'The LORD has sought out a man after his own heart." 1 Samuel 13:14.

[9]   "Do not be overcome by evil, but overcome evil with good." (Romans 12:21)

[10]   Romans 12:15

[11]   Jürgen Moltmann wrote, "Only those who are capable of joy can feel pain at their own and other people's suffering. A man who can laugh can also weep. "Jürgen Moltmann, Theology and Joy (London: SCM Press, LTD, 1973), p. 52. Similarly, Barth wrote "It

is a matter of the proof of our joy in the fact that our capacity for enjoyment shows itself to be also a capacity for suffering." *Church Dogmatics*, Vol. III, Part 4, p. 384.

[12] Robert C. Roberts, *Spirituality and Human Emotion*, (Grand Rapids: William B. Eerdmans Publishing Co., 1982), p. 25.

[13] James Gilman calls sorrow and joy the "empathic virtues" of love. See James E. Gilman, *Fidelity of Heart: An Ethic of Christian Virtue* (Oxford: Oxford University Press, 2001), pp. 53ff.

[14] "But let him who glories glory in this, that he understands and knows me, that I am the LORD who practice steadfast love, justice, and righteousness in the earth; for in these things I delight, says the LORD." (Jeremiah 9:24)

[15] See:

> He has showed you, O man, what is good;
>   and what does the LORD require of you
> but to do justice, and to love kindness,
>   and to walk humbly with your God? (Micah 6:8)

[16] "Blessed are those who mourn, for they shall be comforted." (Matthew 5:4)

[17] ". . . as sorrowful, yet always rejoicing; as poor, yet making many rich; as having nothing, and yet possessing everything." (2 Corinthians 6:10)

[18] Romans 12:15

[19] Gilman, *Fidelity of the Heart*, p. 60.

[20] Hebrews 12:2

[21] This episode is captured in all four of the Gospels. See Matthew 21:12-13; Mark 11:15-17; Luke 19:45-46; John 2:13-17.

[22] "Jesus wept." (John 11:35)

[23] "Blessed are those who mourn, for they shall be comforted." (Matthew 5:4)

CHAPTER 5: KINGDOM ADVENTURES

1 Where does this spiritual vision come from? Contemplation. See my *River of Delights: Quenching Your Thirst for Joy,, Volume 1*, Chapter 6, "Joy and the Word of God, Part 2."

2 Os Guiness, *God in the Dark: The Assurance of Faith Beyond a Shadow of Doubt* (Wheaton, Illinois: Crossway Books, 1996), pp. 200-201.

John Eldredge has written:

> One of the most poisonous of all Satan's whispers is simply, "Things will never change." That lie kills expectation, trapping our heart forever in the present. To keep desire alive and flourishing, we must renew our vision for what lies ahead. Things will not always be like this. Jesus has promised to "make all things new." Eye has not seen, ear has not heard all that God has in store for his lovers, which does not mean "we have no clue so don't even try to imagine," but rather, you cannot outdream God. Desire is kept alive by imagination, the antidote to resignation.

John Eldredge, *The Sacred Romance: Drawing Closer to the Heart of God* (Nashville, TN: Thomas Nelson, Inc., 1997) p. 156.

3 Madeleine L'Engle, *Walking on Water: Reflections on Faith and Art* (Wheaton, IL: Harold Shaw Publishers, 1980), p. 67.

4 1 Corinthians 2:3

5 "And when they could not find them, they dragged Jason and some of the brothers before the city authorities, shouting, 'These men who have turned the world upside down have come here also.'" (Acts 17:6)

6 Nehemiah 8:10

7 Proverbs 31:25

8 In *Path of Life*, I described courageous joy this way:

> Like hopeful joy, this is a joy that faces the future but with a different nuance. It is a confident joy even in the face of danger. It is found in the virtuous woman of Proverbs 31, "Strength and dignity are her clothing, and she laughs at the time to come." It is a joy that defies any challenge the future may bring.

This joy is found again and again in New Testament exhortations, captured in the language of the King James Version: Be of good cheer! And translated in modern versions, Cheer up! Take heart! Take courage! And Have courage!

Rick Howe, *Path of Life: Finding the Joy You've Always Longed For* (Boulder, CO: University Ministries Press, Revised Edition, 2017), p. 33.

[9]   See, for example:

Blessed are those who are persecuted for righteousness' sake, for theirs is the kingdom of heaven. (Matthew 5:10)

Rejoice and be glad, for your reward is great in heaven, for so they persecuted the prophets who were before you. (Matthew 5:12)

Then they left the presence of the council, rejoicing that they were counted worthy to suffer dishonor for the name. (Acts 5:41)

[10] Taken from Cal Samra, *The Joyful Christ: The Healing Power of Humor* (San Francisco: Harper & Row Publishers, 1986), p. 93.

[11] Ibid., pp. 93-94.

[12] Ibid., p. 96.

[13] Ibid.

[14] Philip Shaff, History of the Christian Church (Grand Rapids: Eerdmans Publishing Co., 1910, reprint. 1974), Vol. VI, p. 382.

[15] Ecclesiastes 4:9-10: "Two are better than one, because they have a good reward for their toil. For if they fall, one will lift up his fellow. But woe to him who is alone when he falls and has not another to lift him up!"

[16] That we must look for agents of the Kingdom in the Church is an irony, but it just is the case that not everyone who sits in a pew is committed to the Kingdom. We must look for them.

[17] The risen Christ gave these encouraging words to the apostle Paul when he was in the city of Corinth and must have felt that he was alone in his spiritual commitments: "And the Lord said to Paul one night in a vision, 'Do not be afraid, but go on speaking and do not be silent, for I am with you, and no one will attack you to harm you, for I have many in this city who are my people.'" (Acts 18:9-10)

[18] The distinction between allies and co-belligerents was made popular by Francis Schaeffer.

[19] Mark 12:34

[20] See the following:

> We want you to know, brothers, about the grace of God that has been given among the churches of Macedonia, for in a severe test of affliction, their abundance of joy and their extreme poverty have overflowed in a wealth of generosity on their part. For they gave according to their means, as I can testify, and beyond their means, of their own accord, begging us earnestly for the favor of taking part in the relief of the saints – and this, not as we expected, but they gave themselves first to the Lord and then by the will of God to us. Accordingly, we urged Titus that as he had started, so he should complete among you this act of grace. But as you excel in everything – in faith, in speech, in knowledge, in all earnestness, and in our love for you – see that you excel in this act of grace also. I say this not as a command, but to prove by the earnestness of others that your love also is genuine. For you know the grace of our Lord Jesus Christ, that though he was rich, yet for your sake he became poor, so that you by his poverty might become rich. And in this matter I give my judgment: this benefits you, who a year ago started not only to do this work but also to desire to do it. So now finish doing it as well, so that your readiness in desiring it may be matched by your completing it out of what you have. For if the readiness is there, it is acceptable according to what a person has, not according to what he does not have. For I do not mean that others should be eased and you burdened, but that as a matter of fairness your abundance at the present time should supply their need, so that their abundance may supply your need, that there may be fairness. (2 Corinthians 8:1-14)

> Now it is superfluous for me to write to you about the ministry for the saints, for I know your readiness, of which I boast about you to the people of Macedonia, saying that Achaia has been ready since last year. And your zeal has stirred up most of them. But I am sending the brothers so that our boasting about you may not prove empty in this matter, so that you may be ready, as I said you would be. Otherwise, if some Macedonians come with me and find that you are not ready, we would be humiliated – to say nothing of you – for being so confident. So I thought it necessary to urge the brothers to go on ahead to you and arrange in advance for the gift you have promised, so that it may be ready as a willing gift, not as an exaction.

> The point is this: whoever sows sparingly will also reap sparingly, and whoever sows bountifully will also reap bountifully. Each one must give as he has decided in his heart, not reluctantly or under compulsion, for God loves a cheerful giver. And God is able to make all grace abound to you, so that having all sufficiency in all things at all times, you may abound in every good work. As it is written,

> > "He has distributed freely, he has given to the poor;
> > his righteousness endures forever."

He who supplies seed to the sower and bread for food will supply and multiply your seed for sowing and increase the harvest of your righteousness. You will be enriched in every way to be generous in every way, which through us will produce thanksgiving to God. For the ministry of this service is not only supplying the needs of the saints but is also overflowing in many thanksgivings to God. By their approval of this service, they will glorify God because of your submission that comes from your confession of the gospel of Christ, and the generosity of your contribution for them and for all others, while they long for you and pray for you, because of the surpassing grace of God upon you. Thanks be to God for his inexpressible gift! (2 Corinthians 9:1-15)

[21] Mark 9:40

[22] A local church's involvement in social action (which is what people outside the Church would likely call it), working side-by-side with non-Christian organizations, and even governmental agencies, can turn heads, change minds, and shatter popular stereotypes of Christians. It can create a new openness to the gospel of the Kingdom, and opportunities for Kingdom influence. I have seen it happen in our church (Calvary Bible Church) and our community (Boulder, Colorado). Please see the book *The Externally Focused Church* (Loveland, CO: Group Publishing Co., 2004) by Rick Rusaw and Eric Swanson, two local Christian leaders who have been in the vanguard of this effort.

CHAPTER 6: LIVING IN THE KINGDOM

[1] Luke 22:42

[2] "A jar full of sour wine stood there, so they put a sponge full of the sour wine on a hyssop branch and held it to his mouth. When Jesus had received the sour wine, he said, 'It is finished,' and he bowed his head and gave up his spirit." (John 19:29-30)

[3] Mark 8:34

[4] Romans 12:1

[5] 2 Corinthians 5:14-15

[6] Matthew 6:24; Luke 16:13

[7] See:

And as he was setting out on his journey, a man ran up and knelt before him and asked him, "Good Teacher, what must I do to inherit eternal life?" And Jesus said to him, "Why do you call me good? No one is good except God alone. You know the commandments: 'Do not murder, Do not commit adultery, Do not steal, Do not bear false witness, Do not defraud, Honor your father and mother.'" And he said to him, "Teacher, all these I have kept from my youth." And Jesus, looking at him, loved him, and said to him, "You lack one thing: go, sell all that you have and give to the poor, and you will have treasure in heaven; and come, follow me." Disheartened by the saying, he went away sorrowful, for he had great possessions. And Jesus looked around and said to his disciples, "How difficult it will be for those who have wealth to enter the kingdom of God! (Mark 10:17-23)

[8]   See:

And everyone who has left houses or brothers or sisters or father or mother or children or lands, for my name's sake, will receive a hundredfold and will inherit eternal life. (Matthew 19:29)

Jesus said, "Truly, I say to you, there is no one who has left house or brothers or sisters or mother or father or children or lands, for my sake and for the gospel." (Mark 10:29)

[9]   Ibid.

[10]   Matthew 21:43

[11]   See:

And I, when I came to you, brothers, did not come proclaiming to you the testimony of God with lofty speech or wisdom. For I decided to know nothing among you except Jesus Christ and him crucified. And I was with you in weakness and in fear and much trembling, and my speech and my message were not in plausible words of wisdom, but in demonstration of the Spirit and of power, so that your faith might not rest in the wisdom of men but in the power of God. (1 Corinthians 2:1-5)

[12]   Galatians 6:10

[13]   "The poor you will always have with you." (Matthew 26:11; Mark 14:7)

[14]   See:

So Jesus said to them, "Truly, truly, I say to you, the Son can do nothing of his own accord, but only what he sees the Father doing. For whatever the Father does, that the Son does likewise." (John 5:19)

I can do nothing on my own. As I hear, I judge, and my judgment is just, because I seek not my own will but the will of him who sent me. (John 5:30)

[15]   Ephesians 2:10

www.ingramcontent.com/pod-product-compliance
Lightning Source LLC
Chambersburg PA
CBHW061754020426
42331CB00006B/1478